THE THAI
HOME KITCHEN

Traditional Home-Style Recipes That Capture The Flavors And Memories Of Thailand|

Full-Color Picture Premium Edition

SUNISA KHADPO

Table of Contents

Introduction

Every social event in Thailand includes food, which usually acts as the reason for the gathering itself. Since Thai cuisine was introduced to American diners in the 1960s and 1970s, it has grown to be a restaurant favorite because of its exquisite balancing of five flavors: salty, sweet, bitter, sour, and spicy. It's currently a more popular takeaway choice than pizza in several places. Nothing is more relaxing than ordering Thai cuisine, relaxing on the couch, and 'Netflixing' after a long day at work.

I remember watching my mother cook a lot as a child. My parents are Thai and American, and I was born in the United States. My mother was a talented chef who was well-known among her friends not just for her Thai cuisine but also for her English dishes. She had to prepare American cuisine when she arrived in America, but she still kept her love for Thai food. Most of the time, she would cook Thai food for herself, and the rest of the family ate more American-type foods. When I was growing up, Mom's food always had a different appearance and scent, and to me, it always seemed strange and terrible.

When I was 19, I moved to New Jersey for high school and lived with my aunt, who worked at a Thailand Restaurant. I lived there for several years and grew quite familiar with the Thai manner of cooking and eating, from breakfast to midnight snacks and everything in between.

After finishing university, I returned home for a long stay with my family, during which my parents started a Thai restaurant, and I helped my mother with purchasing ingredients, designing the menu, and serving the customers. This experience taught me which Thai meals are most popular with Americans and how to adapt the traditional Thai food to the context of accessible ingredients and popular tastes.

As I got older and spent more time away from home and relatives, I became more and more inspired to create the Thai food that my mother and aunt used to make, including Thai red curry kabocha squash, mango salad, Thai chicken tacos, Thai coconut pancakes, papaya salad, etc., and all of our favorite snacks, like chicken lettuce wraps, fresh spring rolls with peanut sauce, supreme Thai ribs, roasted chilly dip with pig rinds and many more.

Whenever I went home to see family, I would bring back as many cookbooks as I could carry, as well as whatever Thai kitchen items I could fit into my baggage. The entire home would stink like fried garlic and fish sauce. A love of food is an endless quest for exploration. Something new is constantly waiting around the corner, and without having tasted the flavors, spices, and calming sensations of my mother's cooking, I cannot picture what my life would be like today.

Thai dishes are a fascinating and delicate mix of tastes that delightfully blend together to produce a carnival of flavors for your taste receptors. These tastes complement each other to create an exquisite dish with a broad range of rich and delectable flavor profiles that can easily captivate anybody who eats Thai food. By offering "pick-your-protein" and "pick-your-spice-level" menus, American Thai restaurants have, perhaps unwittingly, created a situation in which even ardent Thai-food devotees are unfamiliar with how these dishes are typically prepared in Thailand, and they end up losing that all-important balance between the five flavors. Furthermore, many of the simple-yet-satisfying staples that Thai people cook at home are rarely available on Thai takeout menus. Even if you have limited access to Asian products, preparing your own Thai food may bring you much closer to the "genuine thing."

Another, perhaps surprising, reason for creating your own Thai cuisine is that it is sometimes the only way to achieve more authentic Thai flavors. Thai restaurants in the United States frequently serve foods that are not genuinely Thai at all or that have been so Westernized that purists would not consider them authentic. This is to cater to palates that have been educated by the prominence of Chinese American restaurants.

This book will guide you through the process of visiting Asian marketplaces, filling your pantry and kitchen with the ingredients needed for Thai food, and explaining popular Thai culinary techniques. It includes everything you need to become an expert Thai cook, including useful ideas and shortcuts, as well as recommendations for substitutes where necessary. Once you've mastered it, you might never look at a takeaway menu again!

Chapter 1
Basics of Thai Food

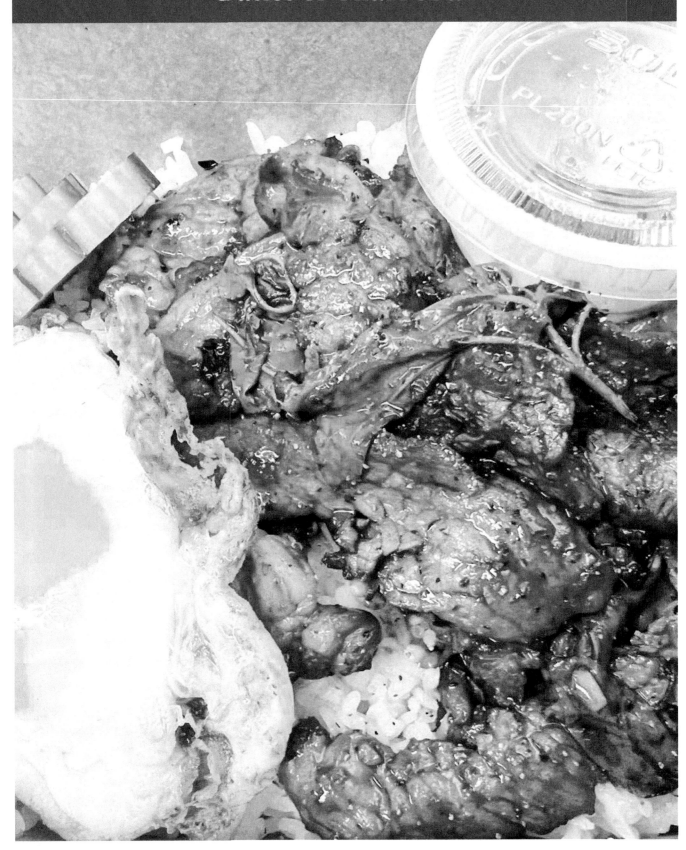

A Brief History, the Thai Food Culture

Thailand's culinary history dates back thousands of years. The Thai people created the Siamese cuisine's foundational ingredients—rice, local vegetables, fragrant herbs, and spicily pungent garlic and pepper—as early as the 13th century.

Thailand has a population of around 60 million people and is roughly the size of France. Myanmar, Laos, Cambodia, and Malaysia are its immediate neighbors. Many ingredients are shared by each cuisine but are frequently employed in completely different ways as a result of commerce between these and other nations in the region, easily proving the notion that food has no borders or limits. While there is regional cooking in Thailand, Thai restaurants often produce and serve well-known meals that they know their customers would appreciate.

Thai food has had a lengthy and delicate evolution, including historical and culinary influences from China. Thai people borrowed dry spices from Arab and Indian traders, such as cumin, nutmeg, coriander, cloves, and turmeric, which are used in Thai Mussaman Curry. This gave a new depth to the efforts of the royal household's outstanding cooks, resulting in one of the world's most exciting cuisines. The chili, which the Portuguese brought East, was maybe the most significant import. Its importance in Thai cooking is unquestionable, but it is the inventive manner the many tastes are combined that distinguishes Thai food.

The tastes, textures, and fragrances of Thai food are its three key charms. Red and green hot bird's eye chilies; creamy coconut; cilantro/coriander; basil leaves, with their aniseed aroma; pine-like galangal; heavenly lemon grass; torn lime leaves; limes for drinks or wedges to wiggle over dishes; pungent kapi, with no fishy taste but GI crunchy green vegetables with unripe fruits for salads, such as green mango, curried meats, and meltingly tender deep-fried fish. The perfume of lemongrass and lime leaves, or curry paste combined with coconut milk, is enough to pique one's interest.

Threads of Indian food may also be seen in the complex tapestry of Thai cuisine. The wet spice pastes are similar to Southern Indian masalas, which always include the three Cs of eastern cooking: coconut, chile, and coriander/cilantro.

Basic Principles to Know when Making A Thai Recipe

It is essential to taste the meal as you cook or prepare it since making Thai food is all about finding the perfect harmony of the five flavors. The flavor may be significantly changed by using different soy sauces, curry pastes, chilies, etc. You will get the ideal balance for your tastes by nibbling while cooking.

The trick is to adjust the recipes to your tastes. When ordering a Thai dish, you may frequently select the popular sauces and the primary component of your choosing. You can follow the same steps while preparing these dishes. For instance, I utilized popular major components like chicken and beef in the traditional curries, but you are welcome to substitute them for prawns or any other protein you desire.

It's also possible to replace other veggies for the ones stated in the recipes. If a recipe uses baby sweetcorn and a variety of basil, but you are unable to find these items, substitute them with other preferred alternatives. Chefs have had to use what was readily available as Thai cuisine spread around the globe. You are free to follow suit.

STOCKING UP

I suggest picking out a few recipes you want to attempt and writing down the necessary items before going on your first ingredient shopping trip. In this manner, you will always have everything you require on hand and won't need to frequently visit the store. The majority of the ingredients may be purchased from supermarkets, however, some must be ordered online or from a local Chinese or Thai market. These things will aid in your Thai cooking experience if you keep them at hand.

SPECIAL EQUIPMENT

Everything you need for these recipes is probably already in your possession. Having said that, you might want to think about getting the following if you're looking to advance your Thai cooking.

1. Large carbon steel wok (for gas burners only)
2. Large non-stick wok (for gas or electric hobs)
3. Steamer for sticky rice
4. Sharp chef's knife
5. Deep-fat fryer
6. Cheese grater
7. Mandoline
8. Granite pestle

PREPARATION IS KEY

The manner in which food is prepared in a formal setting is another important aspect of Thai cuisine. The way the food is presented and the attention to detail are both crucial components of the meal. Even if a dish has mouthwatering flavors, it still needs to look good. This recognizes how highly regarded Thai food and its components are. Serving platters are adorned with fruits and vegetables carved into flowers, and stir-fries prepared in the form of a palace include elegantly carved vegetables. The presentation of Thai food is among the best in the world. Food demands more than just culinary prowess; it also needs to look attractive.

THE FLAVORS ARE ESSENTIAL, IT'S A CULTURE.

A meal can have one or more of the five primary flavors present in Thai cuisine. On the other hand, most Thai dishes aren't considered to be good unless they have all five elements. Despite its spiciness, Thai food ensures that all flavors are prominent and well-balanced.

People eat leisurely and really appreciate their food in Thailand since meals are an opportunity to spend time with friends and family. A variety of meat and seafood dishes, as well as vegetables, noodles, and soup, would likely be included in a dinner prepared or eaten by a group of Thai people. Except for the soup, which may be requested individually and is served in individual bowls, everything is shared. Fresh fruit can be served as an easy dessert, such as pineapple or any of the several tropical fruits that are abundant in this country. There are several options,

including rice cakes, rice dumplings encased in coconut, grass jelly, and bean desserts.

ESSENTIAL INGREDIENTS

Some Thai ingredients could be hard to locate based on where you live and shop. You can get all of the ingredients featured in this book online or through independent Thai and Chinese stores. You can still make delicious Thai food using other, maybe easier-to-find, goods if you wish to attempt the recipes, but you will need to find the components specified in the recipes to get the true Thai flavor. What follows are the items you'll need for this cookbook.

Wet ingredients: Thai fish sauce (compared to other types of fish sauce, Thai fish sauce has a tendency to taste saltier), seasoning sauce, light soy sauce, dark soy sauce, oyster sauce, and fermented bean paste.

Dry ingredients: rice noodles, rice paper, Chinese egg noodles, glass noodles (cellophane noodles or mung bean noodles), palm sugar, dried red bird's eye chilies, tapioca starch/flour, rice flour, plain (all-purpose) flour, peanuts, and cashews.

Fresh and frozen ingredients: garlic, ginger, galangal, red and green bird's eye chilies, mint leaves, red spur chilies, coriander, spring roll wrappers, wonton wrappers, and firm tofu.

Canned and bottled ingredients: salted turnip (Chinese or Thai brands), shrimp paste, condensed milk, thick coconut milk.

The quantity of ingredients utilized in this cookbook suits my preferences. If you find the flavor to be either too strong or too mild, feel free to adjust any flavoring component to your own preference. Starting with less is usually a smart idea because once added, the spice cannot be taken out. Once you've prepared a dish once or twice, you'll know the proportions you need to add for the greatest outcomes.

Chapter 2
Snacks and Appetizers

3-Flavor Rice Sticks

Prep time: 5 minutes | Cook time: 10 minutes | Serves 4-6

- 1 pound rice sticks, broken into 3-inch segments
- Cayenne pepper to taste
- Curry powder to taste
- Salt to taste
- Vegetable oil for frying

1. Pour 2 to 3 inches of vegetable oil into a big frying pan and heat to 350 degrees. Fry the rice sticks in batches (ensuring not to overcrowd the pan), turning them swiftly as they puff up.
2. After they stop crackling in the oil, move the puffed sticks to paper towels to drain.
3. While the rice sticks are still hot, drizzle salt on 1 batch; drizzle a second batch with curry powder; and a third batch with cayenne pepper to taste.

Basil and Shrimp Wedges

Prep time: 5 minutes | Cook time: 10 minutes | Serves 4-6

- ½ cup julienned basil
- ½ pound cooked salad shrimp
- 1 green onion, trimmed and thinly cut
- 1 teaspoon fish sauce
- 1½ teaspoons vegetable oil, divided
- 2 tablespoons water
- 4 eggs
- Salt and pepper to taste

1. Put 1 teaspoon of the vegetable oil in a sauté pan on moderate heat. Put in the shrimp and green onion, and sauté until the shrimp are warmed through, roughly two minutes. Put in the basil and fish sauce and cook for 1 more minute. Set aside.
2. In a big container, whisk together the eggs, water, and salt and pepper, then mix in the shrimp mixture.
3. Put the remaining ½ teaspoon of vegetable oil in an omelet pan on moderate heat. Put in the egg mixture and cook until the omelet starts to brown. Turn over the omelet and carry on cooking until set.
4. To serve, slide the omelet onto a serving plate and cut it into wedges. Serve with a Thai dipping sauce of your choice.

Chicken, Shrimp, and Beef Satay
Prep time: 5 minutes | Cook time: 8 minutes | Serves 1

- Chicken
- 1 recipe Peanut Dipping Sauce
- 1 recipe Thai Marinade
- 3 whole boneless, skinless chicken breasts, cut into lengthy strips about ½-inch wide

1. Thread the chicken strips onto presoaked bamboo skewers or onto metal skewers. Put the skewers in a flat pan and cover with marinade. Marinate the chicken in your fridge overnight.
2. Cook the skewers on the grill or under the broiler, coating and turning them until they are thoroughly cooked, approximately six to eight minutes.
3. Serve with the peanut sauce for dipping.

Shrimp
Prep time: 20 minutes | Cook time: 10 minutes | Serves 4-6

- 1 recipe Peanut Dipping Sauce
- 1 recipe Thai Marinade
- 24 big shrimp, shelled and deveined

1. Thread the shrimp onto presoaked bamboo skewers or onto metal skewers (about 3 shrimp per skewer). Put the skewers in a flat pan and cover with marinade. Marinate the shrimp for minimum fifteen minutes, but no longer than an hour.
2. Cook the skewers on the grill or under the broiler, coating and turning them frequently until just opaque, approximately three to four minutes.
3. Serve with the peanut sauce for dipping.

Beef

Prep time: 5 minutes | Cook time: 8 minutes | Serves 1

- 1 recipe Thai Marinade
- 1 recipe Peanut Dipping Sauce
- 1-1½ pounds sirloin steak, fat and sinew removed, cut into ½-inch-wide strips

1. Thread the beef strips onto presoaked bamboo skewers or onto metal skewers. Put the skewers in a flat pan and cover with marinade. Marinate the beef in your fridge overnight.
2. Cook the skewers on the grill or under the broiler, coating and turning them frequently until done to your preference, approximately six to eight minutes for medium.
3. Serve with the peanut sauce for dipping.

Chinese-Style Dumplings

Prep time: 15 minutes | Cook time: 10 minutes | Serves 15-20

- ¼ cup sticky rice flour
- ¼ cup tapioca flour
- ½ cup water
- 1 cup rice flour
- 1 tablespoon soy sauce
- 1 teaspoon vegetable oil
- 2 cups chives, cut into ½–inch lengths

1. In a moderate-sized-sized deep cooking pan, mix together the sticky rice flour, the rice flour, and the water. Turn the heat to moderate and cook, stirring continuously until the mixture has the consistency of glue. (If the mixture becomes too sticky, decrease the heat to low.) Take away the batter from the heat and swiftly mix in the tapioca flour. Set aside to cool completely.In the meantime, put in the vegetable oil to a frying pan big enough to easily hold the chives, and heat on high. Put in the chives and the soy sauce. Stir-fry the chives just until they wilt. Be careful not to let the chives cook excessively. Turn off the heat and save for later.
2. Once the dough has reached room temperature, check its consistency. If it is too sticky to work with, add a little extra tapioca flour.
3. To make the dumplings, roll the batter into balls an inch in diameter. Using your fingers, flatten each ball into a disk approximately four inches across. Ladle approximately 1 tablespoon of the chives into the middle of each disk. Fold the disk in half and pinch the edges together to make a halfmoon-shaped packet.
4. Put the dumplings in a prepared steamer for five to 8 minutes or until the dough is cooked. Serve with a spicy dipping sauce of your choice.

Thai Pork on Toast

Prep time: 20 minutes | Cook time: 30 minutes | Serves 4

- 14 bread slices
- 2 tablespoons chopped coriander stalks
- 1 tablespoon soy sauce
- ½ teaspoon brown sugar
- ½ pound minced pork
- 4 garlic cloves, minced
- 1 egg
- 1 teaspoon corn flour
- 2 tablespoons coriander leaves
- Salt, to taste

1. Before cooking, heat the baking oven to 150 degrees F.
2. In a blender, process the garlic cloves and coriander stalks until well blended.
3. In a bowl, beat the egg and add pork. Whisk together to coat.
4. Add sugar, coriander paste, corn flour, soy sauce, and salt in the egg mixture and mix well.
5. Spread the mixture on bread slices and add coriander leaves on top.
6. Toast the slices in baking oven for about 30 minutes.
7. Remove and serve. Enjoy!

Thai Pork Meatball Skewers

Prep time: 15 minutes | Cook time: 30 minutes | Serves 2

- ½ pound minced pork
- ½ cup steamed rice
- ½ tablespoon ground black pepper
- ½ garlic head, minced
- Salt, to taste

1. In a bowl, add garlic, rice, salt, pork, and pepper and mix well.
2. Divide the mixture and form them into balls. Place into a zip-lock bag.
3. Let the meat balls to ferment at room temperature for 72 hours.
4. On skewers, thread the meat balls.
5. Grill the skewers for 30 minutes.
6. Serve and enjoy!

Thai Shrimp and Sweetcorn Cakes

Prep time: 15 minutes | Cook time: 10 minutes | Serves 4

- 2 cups sweetcorn
- 2 eggs
- 4 tablespoons chopped coriander
- 2 tablespoons soy sauce
- 2 cups all-purpose flour
- 1 cup peeled shrimp
- 6 garlic cloves, minced
- 6 tablespoons oyster sauce
- Salt and black pepper, to taste

1. In a bowl, add shrimp, garlic, and coriander and mix well.
2. Beat eggs and add flour, sweetcorn, pepper, oyster sauce, soy sauce, and salt. Whisk well.
3. Fry the mixture until golden brown.
4. Remove to a serving bowl. Serve and enjoy!

Thai Fried Turmeric Pork Fillet with Garlic

Prep time: 15 minutes | Cook time: 10 minutes | Serves 4

- 1 pound sliced pork fillet
- 10 garlic cloves, minced
- 1 teaspoon black peppercorn
- 2 tablespoons fresh turmeric
- Salt, to taste

1. In a blender, add turmeric root, black peppercorn, salt, and garlic cloves and blend to form a smooth mixture.
2. Add the pork slices in the mixture and combine well to marinade.
3. Allow the pork to sit for 30 minutes.
4. Then fry until golden brown.
5. Transfer to a serving plate. Serve and enjoy!

Grilled Meatball Skewers
Prep time: 5 minutes | Cook time: 5 minutes | Serves 4

- 32 store-bought Vietnamese-style beef meatballs (bò viên)

1. Prepare a charcoal or gas grill, hibachi, or stovetop grill pan.
2. Arrange 4 meatballs each on 8 (8-inch) bamboo skewers.
3. Grill on the charcoal or gas grill, hibachi, or on a stovetop grill pan until browned, turning frequently to brown evenly on all sides, about 5 minutes total. Be careful not to overcook them, as they are already cooked and just need to be heated through and browned.

Fried Tofu
Prep time: 5 minutes | Cook time: 5 minutes | Serves 16

- Salt
- Neutral oil, such as peanut or refined coconut oil, for frying

1. Slice the tofu in half lengthwise to create two thinner rectangles. Cut each half into quarters, and then cut each quarter diagonally to form small triangles. You should have 16 triangles.
2. Line a baking sheet with 4 layers of paper towels, and arrange the tofu triangles in a single layer on top of the paper towels. Lightly sprinkle the tofu with salt. Cover with 4 more layers of paper towels, and press gently but firmly all over to extract as much water as possible. (I like to then wrap each triangle in another paper towel and gently squeeze in order to dry the sides as well, just before frying.)
3. In a wok or large cast-iron skillet over medium-high heat, heat ½ inch of oil to 375°F (or until a cube of bread browns in the oil in about 30 seconds).
4. Fry the tofu triangles, being careful not to overcrowd them, turning them often with bamboo or wooden chopsticks or tongs to allow them to brown evenly on all sides until light golden brown, about 4 minutes total.
5. Drain well on a paper towel–lined plate. Be careful not to overcook or the triangles will get dry and rubbery.
6. Serve immediately; these are best when piping hot.
7. Serving Suggestion: Serve with Sweet Chili Sauce (here or store-bought) topped with finely chopped roasted peanuts and chopped fresh cilantro, for dipping. Though it's not traditional, they're also great dipped in Satay Peanut Sauce (here).

Cold Sesame Noodles
Prep time: 5 minutes | Cook time: 5 minutes | Serves 2-4

- ¼ cup creamy peanut butter or tahini
- ¼–½ teaspoon dried red pepper flakes
- 1 pound angel hair pasta
- 1 tablespoon grated ginger
- 1–2 green onions, trimmed and thinly cut (not necessary)
- 2 tablespoons rice vinegar
- 2 tablespoons sesame oil

1. Cook the pasta in accordance with package directions. Wash under cold water, then set aside.
2. Vigorously whisk together the rest of the ingredients; pour over pasta, tossing to coat.
3. Decorate using green onion if you wish.

Savory Thai Popcorn
Prep time: 12 minutes | Cook time: 15 minutes | Serves 12

- 4 tablespoons olive oil
- 3 cups salted peanuts, roughly chopped
- 1 cup un-popped popcorns
- ½ cup almond oil
- 4 tablespoons soy sauce
- 2 tablespoons lime zest
- ½ teaspoon baking soda
- 1¼ cups brown sugar
- 6 tablespoons sriracha sauce
- 2 tablespoons lime juice

1. In a large pan, add olive oil and the un-popped popcorn kernels and stir well.
2. Cover the lid of the pan and cook for about 10 minutes until all the popcorn kernel are popped.
3. In another pan, mix together almond oil, brown sugar, soy sauce, lime juice, lime zest, and sriracha and simmer for about 5 minutes.
4. Mixed in the baking soda and the salted peanuts.
5. Serve the popcorns with the sauce mixture.

Chapter 3
Soups

Asian Chicken Noodle Soup

Prep time: 5 minutes | Cook time: 50 minutes | Serves 4-6

- ½ cup chopped onion
- 1 carrot, peeled and julienned
- 1 cup chopped cilantro
- 1 moderate-sized sweet red pepper, seeded and julienned
- 2 cups chicken broth
- 2 star anise
- 2 tablespoons chopped ginger
- 2 tablespoons fish sauce
- 2 tablespoons vegetable oil
- 2 whole boneless, skinless chicken breasts, cut into lengthy strips
- 3 cloves garlic, minced
- 3 ounces snow peas, trimmed
- 4 ounces, cellophane noodles, soaked in boiling water for five minutes and drained
- 5 cups water, divided
- Lemon or lime wedges
- Peanuts, crudely chopped

1. In a big deep cooking pan, heat the oil on high. Put in the onion and sauté until translucent. Put in the ginger, garlic, and cilantro, and sauté for 1 more minute. Mix in the broth and 2 cups of the water. Put in the star anise. Bring to its boiling point, reduce heat, and cover; simmer for twenty minutes to half an hour.
2. In another deep cooking pan, bring the rest of the water to its boiling point. Put in the vegetables and blanch for a minute or until soft-crisp. Drain and run very cold water over the vegetables to stop the cooking process; set aside.
3. Strain the broth into a clean soup pot and bring to its boiling point. Put in the chicken strips and reduce heat. Poach the chicken using low heat until opaque, roughly ten minutes. Put in the cellophane noodles and reserved vegetables, and carry on simmering for two more minutes. Season to taste with fish sauce.
4. To serve, ladle the soup into warm bowls. Drizzle with peanuts and decorate with lime wedge.

Chicken Soup with Lemongrass

Prep time: 5 minutes | Cook time: 20 minutes | Serves 4-6

- ¾ pound boneless, skinless chicken breast, trimmed and slice into bite-sized pieces
- 1 (14-ounce) can unsweetened coconut milk
- 1 (1-inch) piece ginger, cut into 6 pieces
- 1 clove garlic, minced
- 1 medium onion, minced
- 1 stalk lemongrass, trimmed, bruised, and slice into 2 to 3 pieces
- 1 tablespoon vegetable oil
- 2 cups wild or domestic mushrooms, cut into bite-sized pieces (if required)
- 2 tablespoons fish sauce
- 2 teaspoons prepared Red Curry Paste or curry powder
- 3 lime leaves (fresh or dried)
- 4 cups chicken broth
- Juice of 2 limes
- Salt and pepper to taste

1. In a moderate-sized-sized deep cooking pan, mix the oil, onion, and garlic. Cook on moderate heat for a minute. Put in the lemongrass, curry paste, ginger, and lime leaves.
2. Cook while stirring, for about three minutes, then put in the broth. Bring to its boiling point, decrease the heat to moderate, and carry on cooking for ten more minutes.
3. Put in the coconut milk, the chicken pieces, and the mushrooms. Continue to cook for five minutes or until the chicken is done.
4. Mix in the lime juice and fish sauce. Sprinkle salt and pepper to taste.
5. Take away the lemongrass, lime leaves, and ginger pieces before you serve.

Chilled Mango Soup

Prep time: 5 minutes | Cook time: 15 minutes | Serves 2-4

- 1 cup plain yogurt
- 1 tablespoon dry sherry
- 1 teaspoon sugar (not necessary)
- 1½ cups chilled chicken or vegetable broth
- 2 big mangoes, peeled, pitted, and chopped
- Salt and white pepper to taste

1. Put all of the ingredients in a blender or food processor and process until the desired smoothness is achieved. Adjust seasonings.
2. This soup may be served instantly or placed in the fridge until needed. If you do place in your fridge the soup, allow it to sit at room temperature for about ten minutes or so before you serve to take some of the chill off.

Coconut Chicken Soup (Tom Khai Gai)

Prep time: 15 minutes | Cook time: 20 minutes | Serves 4

- ¾ pound boneless chicken meat
- 3 tablespoons vegetable oil
- 2 (14-ounce) cans coconut milk
- 2 tablespoons fresh ginger root, minced
- 4 tablespoons fish sauce
- ½ cup fresh lime juice
- ¼ teaspoon cayenne pepper
- ½ teaspoon ground turmeric
- 2 tablespoons scallions, sliced
- 1 tablespoon fresh cilantro, chopped

1. Cut up your chicken into strips.
2. Take a skillet and place it over medium heat, add oil, and heat it up.
3. Add the chicken strips and sauté them for about 2-3 minutes.
4. Take a pot and bring the coconut milk and water to a boil.
5. Lower down the heat to low.
6. Add ginger, lime juice, fish sauce, turmeric, and cayenne powder.
7. Simmer the chicken for about 10-15 minutes.
8. Sprinkle it with a bit of cilantro and scallions.
9. Serve hot!

Hot and Sour Tom Yum Soup with Shrimp (Tom Yum Goong)

Prep time: 10 minutes | Cook time: 5 minutes | Serves 4

- 4 cups water or basic Thai chicken stock
- 6 (⅛-inch-thick) slices unpeeled fresh galangal, bruised with the butt of a chef's knife, optional
- 3 lemon grass stalks (bottom 3 inches only), bruised with the flat side of a chef's knife
- 2 fresh kaffir lime leaves, optional
- 2 tablespoons roasted chili paste
- 3 tablespoons fish sauce
- 1 cup fresh button mushrooms cut into ¼ -inch slices, or canned straw mushrooms, drained and halved or left whole
- 12 large raw shrimp, deveined, peeled, or impeded, as you prefer; if removing the shell, leave tails on for a nicer presentation
- ¼ cup lime juice, freshly squeezed
- 1 or 2 fresh red Thai bird's-eye chiles, stemmed, seeded, and each thinly sliced lengthwise into 4 strips, optional
- ¼ cup fresh cilantro leaves, for serving

1. Take a medium saucepan and add water, lemon grass, and kaffir lime leaves into it.
2. Cover and bring just to a boil over high heat.
3. Turn the heat to low and simmer for 5 minutes.
4. Remove and discard lemon grass and lime leaves.
5. Stir in the chili paste.
6. Add the mushrooms and simmer for 1 minute.
7. Then add the shrimp and simmer for 1 minute more.
8. Remove from the heat and stir in the lime juice and chiles.
9. Adjust the seasoning, as needed, with additional fish sauce or lime juice.
10. Take a small bowl and sprinkle with cilantro on top.
11. Serve and enjoy!

Hot-And-Sour Tom Yum Soup With Shrimp

Prep time: 10 minutes | Cook time: 5 minutes | Serves 4

- 4 cups water or Basic Thai Chicken Stock (here)
- 6 (⅛-inch-thick) slices unpeeled fresh galangal, bruised with the butt of a chef's knife (optional)
- 3 lemongrass stalks (bottom 3 inches only), bruised with the flat side of a chef's knife
- 2 fresh kaffir lime leaves (optional)
- 2 tablespoons Roasted Chili Paste (here or store-bought)
- 3 tablespoons fish sauce
- 1 cup fresh button mushrooms cut into ¼-inch slices, or canned straw mushrooms, drained and halved or left whole
- 12 large raw shrimp, deveined (peeled or unpeeled, as you prefer; if removing the shell, leave tails on for a nicer presentation)
- ¼ cup freshly squeezed lime juice (or to taste)
- 1 or 2 fresh red Thai bird's-eye chiles, stemmed, seeded, and each thinly sliced lengthwise into 4 strips (optional)
- ¼ cup fresh cilantro leaves, for serving

1. Place the water, galangal (if using), lemongrass, and kaffir lime leaves (if using) in a medium saucepan or Dutch oven. Cover and bring just to a boil over high heat. Turn the heat to low and simmer for 5 minutes.
2. Remove and discard the galangal, lemongrass, and lime leaves at this point if you intend to serve the soup without them (Thais leave them in, but they're just for flavoring, not for eating).
3. Stir in the chili paste until it dissolves, and then stir in the fish sauce. Add the mushrooms, and simmer for 1 minute.
4. Add the shrimp, and simmer for 1 minute more.
5. Remove from the heat and stir in the lime juice and chiles (if using). Adjust the seasoning, as needed, with additional fish sauce or lime juice.
6. Serve immediately in small bowls, sprinkling each serving with cilantro.

Coconut-Galangal Soup
Prep time: 10 minutes | Cook time: 10 minutes | Serves 4

- 2 cups Basic Thai Chicken Stock (here) or water
- 1½ cups coconut milk
- 10 (⅛-inch-thick) slices unpeeled fresh galangal, bruised with the butt of a chef's knife
- 4 kaffir lime leaves, bruised by rolling between your fingers
- 1 stalk lemongrass (bottom 3 inches only), bruised with the flat side of a chef's knife
- 3 tablespoons fish sauce
- ¾ pound boneless, skinless chicken (breast or thigh meat), cut into bitesize pieces (about 2 inches by ½ inch by ⅛ inch)
- 1 cup quartered fresh button mushrooms (optional)
- 1 to 2 fresh red Thai bird's-eye chiles, stemmed, seeded, and thinly sliced lengthwise (optional)
- 2 tablespoons freshly squeezed lime juice
- ½ cup fresh cilantro leaves
- 2 scallions, green part only, sliced crosswise into ¼-inch-thick rings (about 2 tablespoons; optional)

1. In a medium saucepan or Dutch oven over medium heat, bring the stock, coconut milk, galangal, kaffir lime leaves, and lemongrass just to a boil. Turn the heat to low and simmer, covered, for 5 minutes.
2. Remove and discard the galangal, lime leaves, and lemongrass at this point if you intend to serve the soup without them (Thais leave them in, but they're just for flavoring, not for eating).
3. Stir in the fish sauce, chicken, mushrooms (if using), and chiles (if using). Bring back to a simmer over medium heat, and then turn the heat to low and simmer, covered, until the chicken is cooked, about 3 minutes.
4. Remove from the heat and stir in the lime juice. Adjust the seasoning, if necessary, with additional fish sauce and lime juice.
5. Serve immediately in small bowls, sprinkling each serving with cilantro and scallions (if using).

Thai Shrimp Rice Soup
Prep time: 25 minutes | Cook time: 30 minutes | Serves 8

- 6 cups chicken stock
- ½ teaspoon white peppercorns
- ½ pound shrimp, cut into small chunks
- 1 tablespoon soy sauce
- 6 cups cooked jasmine rice
- 6 garlic cloves, minced
- 12 cilantro stems
- 2 tablespoons fish sauce

1. In a food processor, add the garlic, cilantro, and white peppercorns and pulse to form a smooth puree. Use half the puree to marinade shrimps.
2. Sauté the marinated shrimps in a pan and add chicken stock in it.
3. Bring to a boil and pour in the remaining puree in the pot, stirring continuously.
4. Then add rice and cook for about 5 minutes.
5. When cooked, remove from heat. Add fish sauce and soy sauce and stir well to combine.
6. Serve and enjoy!

Refreshing Cucumber Soup

Prep time: 15 minutes | Cook time: 30 minutes | Serves 4

- 2 tablespoons butter
- 2 tablespoons green onion, sliced
- 3 cucumbers, chopped
- ⅓ cup red wine vinegar
- 1-quart chicken broth
- 2 cups water
- 3 hot chile peppers, minced and seeded
- 3 tablespoons fresh parsley, chopped
- 1 tablespoon fresh cilantro, chopped
- 1 tablespoon fish sauce
- 1 teaspoon soy sauce
- Salt as needed
- Pepper as needed
- ½ cup sour cream
- 2 white stalks of lemon grass, bruised
- 1½ inches ginger, sliced

1. Take a deep pan and place it over medium heat.
2. Add butter and allow it to heat up.
3. Add green onions and cook them until tender.
4. Stir in vinegar, cucumber, chicken broth, chile peppers, water, parsley, lemon grass, cilantro, garlic, soy sauce, fish sauce, ginger.
5. Season with some salt and pepper.
6. Simmer it over medium heat until the cucumbers are tender for about 20 minutes.
7. Stir in sour cream and simmer for 10 minutes more. Enjoy!

Thai Chicken Noodle Soup

Prep time: 15 minutes | Cook time: 20 minutes | Serves 2

- 4 ounces dry Chinese noodles
- 1 (14.5-ounce) can chicken broth
- 6 shitake mushrooms, sliced
- 2 green onions, chopped
- 1 skinless and boneless chicken breast half
- 2 eggs

1. Take a bowl of water and bring it to a boil.
2. Stir in noodles and cook until al dente for about 8-10 minutes.
3. Drain the noodles and divide them into two serving bowls.
4. Take a medium-sized saucepan and place it over medium heat.
5. Add chicken broth and bring it to a boil.
6. Add green onions and mushrooms.
7. Cut up the chicken into bite-sized portions and stir it into the broth.
8. Once the broth comes to a boil, crack in the eggs.
9. Keep cooking for about 10 minutes until the chickens are no longer pink, and the eggs are cooked.
10. Pour the chicken soup over the noodle bowls.
11. Enjoy!

Lemony Chicken Soup

Prep time: 5 minutes | Cook time: 30 minutes | Serves 4-6

- ½ cup lemon slices, including peel
- 1 cup straw mushrooms
- 1 tablespoon minced fresh ginger
- 1 whole boneless, skinless chicken breast, poached and shredded
- 1½ cups coconut milk
- 1½ teaspoons fresh hot chili pepper, seeded and chopped
- 1½ teaspoons sugar
- 2 cups chicken broth
- 2 green onions, thinly cut
- 3 tablespoons fish sauce
- 3 teaspoons lemongrass, peeled and chopped

1. Mix the lemon slices, fish sauce, chili pepper, green onion, and sugar in a small glass container; set aside.
2. Mix the coconut milk, chicken broth, lemongrass, mushrooms, and ginger in a deep cooking pan. Bring to its boiling point, reduce heat, and simmer for twenty to twenty-five minutes. Put in the chicken and lemon mixture; heat through.
3. To serve, ladle into warmed bowls.

Exotic Thai Pumpkin Soup

Prep time: 10 minutes | Cook time: 15 minutes | Serves 4

- 1 tablespoon vegetable oil
- 1 tablespoon butter
- 1 chopped garlic clove
- 4 chopped shallots
- 2 small-sized fresh red chili pepper, chopped up
- 1 tablespoon chopped lemon grass
- 2 ⅛ cups chicken stock
- 4 cups peeled and diced pumpkin
- 1 ½ cups unsweetened coconut milk
- 1 bunch fresh basil leaves

1. Take a medium-sized saucepan and place it over low heat.
2. Add oil and heat it up.
3. Add butter and melt.
4. Add garlic, chilies, shallots, lemon grass, and stir until fragrant.
5. Stir in chicken stock, pumpkin, and coconut milk.
6. Bring the mixture to a boil.
7. Cook until the pumpkin is tender.
8. Take a blender and blend the sup in batches until a smooth soup form.
9. Serve the soup with some basil leaves!

Chapter 4
Curries

Thai Monkfish Curry

Prep time: 20 minutes | Cook time: 20 minutes | Serves 4

- 1 teaspoon peanut oil
- 12 finely chopped sweet onion
- 1 chopped red bell pepper
- 3 tablespoons red Thai curry paste
- 1 can (14 oz.) coconut milk
- 12 ounces monkfish, cubed
- 1 teaspoon fish sauce
- 2 teaspoons lime juice
- 2 tablespoons cilantro, chopped

1. In a large sauce pan over medium heat, heat the peanut oil. Cook until the onion is softened and translucent, 3 to 5 minutes. Cook for 3 to 5 minutes more, or until red bell pepper is softened. Cook for 1 minute after adding the curry paste. Pour in the coconut milk and bring to a gentle simmer.
2. When the coconut milk starts to boil, add the cubed monkfish and cook for 7 to 10 minutes, or until the fish is firm and the middle is no longer opaque. Until serving, combine the fish sauce, lime juice, and cilantro.

Traditional Coconut Shrimp Curry

Prep time: 15 minutes | Cook time: 120 minutes | Serves 4

- 1 pound shrimp, with shells
- 3 ¾ cups light coconut milk
- 1 ¾ cups water
- ½ cup Thai red curry sauce
- 2 ½ teaspoons lemon garlic seasoning
- ¼ cup cilantro

1. Add coconut milk, red curry sauce, water, lemon garlic seasoning, and cilantro to your Slow Cooker.
2. Give it a nice stir.
3. Cook on HIGH for 2 hours.
4. Add shrimp and cook for another 15-30 minutes.
5. Garnish with some cilantro and serve!

Authentic Green Curry Prawn

Prep time: 25 minutes | Cook time: 15 minutes | Serves 4

- ½ teaspoon cumin powder
- 1 ½ teaspoons coriander powder
- 1 tablespoon fresh ginger root, minced
- 4 tablespoons minced garlic
- ⅓ cup chopped fresh cilantro
- 2 green chili peppers, chopped
- 3 stalks lemon grass, minced
- 1 lime, zested
- 2 limes, juiced
- 2 teaspoons corn oil
- ¼ cup corn oil
- ½ pound fresh green beans, trimmed
- 1 (7 ounces) can drained baby corn
- 1 teaspoon soy sauce
- 1 can (14 oz.) coconut milk
- ¾ pound medium peeled and deveined shrimp (30-40 per pound)

1. In a food processor, combine cumin, coriander, ginger, garlic, green chili peppers, lemon grass, cilantro, lime juice, lime zest, and 2 tablespoons corn oil.
2. To make a smooth, dense paste, combine all of the ingredients in a food processor. Place aside.
3. In a wide skillet over medium-high heat, heat ¼ cup corn oil. Green beans and baby corn should be cooked and stirred for about 30 seconds.
4. Bring to a boil with the paste, soy sauce, and coconut milk.
5. Reduce the heat to medium and cook for 5 to 7 minutes before adding the shrimp. 3 to 5 minutes, or until the shrimp are bright pink on the outside, and the meat is no longer translucent in the middle.
6. If the sauce becomes too thick, add a splash of water.

Thai Potato Yellow Curry

Prep time: 15 minutes | Cook time: 20-30 minutes | Serves 4

- 1 tablespoon olive oil
- ½ yellow onion, sliced
- 1 pound boneless skinless chicken breasts, diced
- 3 tablespoons yellow curry paste
- 10 baby golden Yukon potatoes, peeled and diced
- 1 14-ounce can coconut cream (similar to coconut milk, but much more decadent)
- ½ cup water
- 2 tablespoons fish sauce (optional)
- ½–¼ tablespoon brown sugar (optional)

1. In a large pot, heat the oil over medium-low heat. Sauté the onions for a few minutes, or until they are fragrant and softened. Cook for 3-5 minutes after adding the chicken and curry paste. Stir in the potatoes to coat with the curry paste.
2. Add the coconut cream and ½ cup of water to the pot and lower down heat, simmer for 20-30 minutes, Until the chicken and potatoes are completely cooked, adding more water as required to achieve the desired sauce consistency.
3. To kick it up a notch, add the fish sauce and brown sugar. Seriously, it's fantastic. Serve with rice.

Classic Thai Pineapple Chicken Curry

Prep time: 10 minutes | Cook time: 50 minutes | Serves 3

- 1 cup cooked jasmine rice
- 2 tablespoons red curry paste
- 1 chicken breast, cut into strips
- 2 tablespoons white sugar
- ¼ red bell pepper, julienned
- ¼ small onion, chopped
- 2 cups water
- ¾ cup coconut milk
- 1½ tablespoons fish sauce
- ½ cup bamboo shoots, drained
- ¼ green bell pepper, julienned
- ½ cup pineapple chunks, drained

1. In a pot, add water and rice and cook for about 25 minutes.
2. Stir in coconut milk, fish sauce, chicken, bamboo shoots, sugar, and red curry paste and cook for 15 minutes.
3. Add green bell pepper, onion, and red bell pepper in the pot and cook for about 10 minutes.
4. Take out and add pineapple chunks and stir well.
5. Serve and enjoy!

Green Curry Paste

Prep time: 5 minutes | Cook time: 40 minutes | Serves 1

- 1 (1-inch) piece ginger, peeled and chopped
- 1 medium onion, chopped
- 1 teaspoon salt
- 1 teaspoon shrimp paste
- 2 green bell peppers, seeded and chopped
- 2 tablespoons vegetable oil
- 2 teaspoons chopped lemongrass
- 2 teaspoons cumin seeds, toasted
- 2–4 green jalapeño chilies, seeded and chopped
- 3 cloves garlic, chopped
- 3 tablespoons coriander seeds, toasted
- 3 teaspoons water
- 4 tablespoons chopped cilantro
- 4 tablespoons Tamarind Concentrate

1. Put all the ingredients in a food processor and pulse until the desired smoothness is achieved. Move to a small deep cooking pan and bring to a simmer on moderate to low heat. Decrease the heat to low and cook, stirring regularly, for five minutes.
2. Mix in 1 cup of water and bring the mixture to its boiling point. Decrease the heat, cover, and simmer for half an hour

Basic Red Gaeng Kua Curry Paste

Prep time: 15 minutes | Cook time: 15 minutes | Serves ½

- 8 to 10 dried red chiles (2 to 3 inches long), stemmed and seeded
- 1 teaspoon salt
- 2 tablespoons finely chopped lemongrass (from the bottom 3 inches of 2 stalks)
- 4 teaspoons finely chopped galangal
- 1 tablespoon cilantro root or stem
- 1 teaspoon kaffir lime zest
- ½ cup thinly sliced shallot (about 2 large shallots)
- ¼ cup thinly sliced garlic (about 4 large cloves)
- 1 teaspoon shrimp paste (optional, but recommended)

1. In a small bowl, soak the chiles in hot water until softened, 10 to 15 minutes.
2. Squeeze the soaked chiles well to remove excess water. In a mortar and pestle or spice grinder, pulverize them together with the salt.
3. In the mortar and pestle or a blender, pound or blend the chiles with the lemongrass, galangal, cilantro root or stem, and kaffir lime zest to form a paste.
4. Add the shallots, garlic, and shrimp paste (if using), and pound or blend again. The final paste should be relatively smooth, with no large chunks or fibers (but a paste made in a mortar will not be as smooth as a machine-made paste).

Choo Chee Curry Paste

Prep time: 15 minutes | Cook time: 15 minutes | Serves ½

- 2 dried red chiles (2 to 3 inches long), stemmed and seeded
- ½ teaspoon salt
- 4 tablespoons toasted coconut flakes (see Note)
- 1 teaspoon white peppercorns
- 4½ teaspoons finely chopped lemongrass (from the bottom 3 inches of 2 stalks)
- 2 teaspoons finely chopped galangal
- ½ teaspoon kaffir lime zest
- ½ teaspoon cilantro root or stem
- ¼ cup thinly sliced shallot (from 1 large shallot)
- 2 tablespoons thinly sliced garlic (about 2 large cloves)
- ½ teaspoon shrimp paste (optional, but recommended)

1. In a small bowl, soak the chiles in hot water until softened, 10 to 15 minutes.
2. Squeeze the soaked chiles well to remove excess water. In a mortar and pestle or spice grinder, pulverize the chiles together with the salt.
3. Add the toasted coconut flakes and white peppercorns, and pound or grind until even. In the mortar and pestle or a blender, pound or blend the chile-coconut mixture with the lemongrass, galangal, kaffir lime zest, and cilantro root or stem to form a paste.
4. Add the shallot, garlic, and shrimp paste (if using), and pound or blend again. The final paste should be relatively smooth, with no large chunks or fibers (but a paste made in a mortar will not be as smooth as a machine-made paste).

Prik Khing Curry Paste

Prep time: 10 minutes | Cook time: 15 minutes | Serves ½

- 4 dried red chiles (2 to 3 inches long), stemmed and seeded
- 1 teaspoon salt
- 1 teaspoon white peppercorns
- 1 tablespoon finely chopped lemongrass (from the bottom 3 inches of 2 stalks)
- 1 tablespoon finely chopped galangal
- 2 teaspoons kaffir lime zest (from 2 or 3 kaffir limes)
- ½ cup thinly sliced shallot (about 2 large shallots)
- ¼ cup thinly sliced garlic (about 4 large cloves)
- 2 teaspoons shrimp paste (optional)

1. In a small bowl, soak the dried chiles in hot water until softened, 10 to 15 minutes.
2. Squeeze the soaked chiles well to remove excess water. In a mortar and pestle or spice grinder, pulverize them together with the salt.
3. Add the peppercorns, and pound or grind to form an even paste.
4. In the mortar and pestle or a blender, pound or blend the chile mixture with the lemongrass, galangal, and kaffir lime zest to form a paste.
5. Add the shallot, garlic, and shrimp paste (if using), and pound or blend again. The final paste should be relatively smooth, with no large chunks or fibers (but a paste made in a mortar will not be as smooth as a machine-made paste).

Jungle Curry Paste

Prep time: 15 minutes | Cook time: 15 minutes | Serves ¼

- 10 dried red chiles (2 to 3 inches long), stemmed and seeded
- 4 to 6 fresh green Thai bird's-eye chiles or 1 to 2 large green jalapeños or serranos, stemmed and chopped
- 1 teaspoon salt
- 2 tablespoons finely chopped lemongrass (from the bottom 3 inches of 4 stalks)
- 1 tablespoon finely chopped galangal
- 1 tablespoon finely chopped fingerroot (grachai; see here)
- ¼ cup thinly sliced shallot (from 1 large shallot)
- 2 tablespoons thinly sliced garlic (about 2 large cloves)
- 1 teaspoon shrimp paste (optional)

1. In a small bowl, soak the dried chiles in hot water until softened, 10 to 15 minutes.
2. Squeeze the soaked chiles well to remove excess water. In a mortar and pestle or blender, pulverize the soaked chiles together with the fresh green chiles and the salt.
3. Add the lemongrass, galangal, and fingerroot, and pound or blend to form a paste.
4. Add the shallot, garlic, and shrimp paste (if using), and pound or blend again. The final paste should be relatively smooth, with no large chunks or fibers (but a paste made in a mortar will not be as smooth as a machine-made paste).

Northern (or Jungle) Curry Paste
Prep time: 5 minutes | Cook time: 15 minutes | Serves 2

- ¼ cup chopped arugula
- ¼ cup chopped chives
- ½ cup chopped mint
- 1 (3-inch) piece ginger, peeled and chopped
- 1 cup chopped basil
- 1 stalk lemongrass, tough outer leaves removed and discarded, inner core minced
- 1 tablespoon shrimp paste
- 12 serrano chilies, seeded and chopped
- 2 tablespoons vegetable oil
- 4 shallots, chopped
- 6–8 Thai bird chilies, seeded and chopped

1. In a moderate-sized-sized sauté pan, heat the oil on medium. Put in shrimp paste, lemongrass, ginger, and shallots, and sauté until shallots start to turn translucent and the mixture is very aromatic.
2. Move the mixture to a food processor and pulse until adding 1 or 2 tablespoons of water to help with the grinding.
3. Put in the rest of the ingredients and more water if required to pulse until crudely mixed.

Red Curry Paste
Prep time: 5 minutes | Cook time: 40 minutes | Serves ½

- 1 (½-inch) piece ginger, finely chopped
- 1 medium onion, chopped
- 1 stalk lemongrass, outer leaves removed and discarded, inner core finely chopped
- 1 teaspoon salt
- 2 garlic cloves, chopped
- 2 tablespoons Tamarind Concentrate
- 2 teaspoons cumin seeds, toasted
- 2 teaspoons paprika
- 3 kaffir lime leaves or the peel of 1 lime, chopped
- 3 tablespoons coriander seeds, toasted
- 3 tablespoons vegetable oil
- 4 tablespoons water
- 6–8 red serrano chilies, seeded and chopped

1. Put all the ingredients in a food processor and pulse until super smooth.
2. Move to a small deep cooking pan and bring to a simmer on moderate to low heat. Decrease the heat to low and cook, stirring regularly, for five minutes.
3. Mix in 1 cup of water and bring the mixture to its boiling point. Decrease the heat, cover, and simmer thirty minutes.

Southern (or Massaman) Curry Paste
Prep time: 5 minutes | Cook time: 40 minutes | Serves 1

- ¼ teaspoon ground cinnamon
- ¼ teaspoon whole black peppercorns
- ½ teaspoon cardamom seeds, toasted
- 1 (1-inch) piece ginger, peeled and minced
- 1 stalk lemongrass, tough outer leaves removed and discarded, inner core finely chopped
- 1 teaspoon lime peel
- 1 teaspoon salt
- 1 teaspoon shrimp paste (not necessary)
- 2 tablespoons coriander seeds, toasted
- 2 tablespoons vegetable oil
- 2 teaspoons brown sugar
- 2 teaspoons cumin seeds, toasted
- 2 whole cloves
- 3 tablespoons Tamarind Concentrate
- 3 tablespoons water
- 6–8 big dried red chilies (often called California chilies), soaked in hot water for five minutes and drained

1. Put all ingredients in a food processor and pulse until the desired smoothness is achieved.
2. Move to a small deep cooking pan and bring to a simmer on moderate to low heat. Decrease the heat to low and cook, stirring regularly, for five minutes.
3. Mix in 1 cup of water and bring the mixture to its boiling point. Decrease the heat, cover, and simmer thirty minutes

Chapter 5
Meat Recipes

Green Curry Beef

Prep time: 5 minutes | Cook time: 15 minutes | Serves 4-6

- ¼ cup (or to taste) Green Curry Paste
- ¼ cup brown sugar
- ¼ cup fish sauce
- 1 cup basil
- 1 pound eggplant (Japanese, Thai, or a combination), cut into ¼-inch slices
- 1½ pounds sirloin, cut into fine strips
- 2 cans coconut milk, thick cream separated from the milk
- 6 serrano chilies, stemmed, seeded, and cut in half along the length

1. Put the thick cream from the coconut milk and the curry paste in a big soup pot and stir until blended. Put on moderate to high heat and bring to its boiling point. Decrease the heat and simmer for two to three minutes.
2. Put in the beef and the coconut milk, stirring to blend. Return the mixture to a simmer.
3. Put in the sugar and the fish sauce, stirring until the sugar dissolves, approximately 2 minutes.
4. Put in the eggplant and simmer for one to two minutes.
5. Put in the serrano chilies and cook one minute more.
6. Turn off the heat and mix in the basil.

Curried Beef and Potato Stew

Prep time: 5 minutes | Cook time: 85 minutes | Serves 4

- ¼ cup Tamarind Concentrate
- ½ cup brown sugar
- ½ cup unsalted roasted peanuts, chopped
- ½–¾ cup prepared Massaman Curry Paste
- 1 big onion, chopped
- 1 big russet potato, peeled and slice into bite-sized cubes
- 1 cup chopped fresh pineapple
- 1½ pounds beef stew meat, cut into bite-sized cubes
- 2 (14-ounce) cans coconut milk
- 2–3 tablespoons vegetable oil
- 7 tablespoons fish sauce
- Jasmine rice, cooked in accordance with package directions

1. Heat the oil in a big soup pot on moderate to high heat. Once the oil is hot, brown the meat on all sides. Put in the onion and cook until translucent, approximately two to three minutes.
2. Put in enough water to just cover the meat and onions. Bring to its boiling point, reduce heat, cover, and simmer for thirty to 60 minutes.
3. Put in the potatoes and carry on simmering for fifteen more minutes. (The potatoes will not be fairly thoroughly cooked now.)
4. Strain the solids from the broth, saving for later both.
5. In another soup pot, mix the coconut milk with the curry paste until well mixed. Bring the contents to a simmer on moderate to high heat and cook for two to three minutes.
6. Put in the reserved meat and potato mixture, the sugar, fish sauce, and tamarind, stirring until the sugar dissolves. Put in some of the reserved broth to thin the sauce to desired consistency.
7. Mix in the pineapple and carry on simmering until the potatoes are thoroughly cooked.
8. To serve, place some Jasmine rice in the center of individual serving plates and spoon the stew over the top. Decorate using the chopped peanuts.

Hot and Sour Beef

Prep time: 5 minutes | Cook time: 10 minutes | Serves 1-2

- 1 green onion, trimmed and thinly cut
- 1 tablespoon dark, sweet soy sauce
- 1 tablespoon fish sauce
- 1 tablespoon lime juice
- 1 teaspoon chopped cilantro
- 1 teaspoon dried chili powder
- 1 teaspoon honey
- 1½ pound sirloin steak
- 3 tablespoons chopped onion
- Salt and pepper to taste

1. Make the sauce by meticulously combining the first 8 ingredients; set aside.
2. Flavour the steak with salt and pepper, then grill or broil it to your preferred doneness. Take away the steak from the grill, cover using foil, and allow to rest for five to ten minutes.
3. Thinly slice the steak, cutting across the grain.
4. Position the pieces on a serving platter or on 1 or 2 dinner plates. Ladle the sauce over the top. Serve with rice and a side vegetable.

Fresh Thai Beef and Peanut Butter Dish

Prep time: 10 minutes | Cook time: 10 minutes | Serves 4

- 1 cup beef stock
- 4 tablespoons peanut butter
- ¼ teaspoon garlic powder
- ¼ teaspoon onion powder
- 1 tablespoon coconut amino
- 1½ teaspoons lemon pepper
- 1 pound beef steak, cut into strips
- Salt and pepper to taste
- 1 green bell pepper, seeded and chopped
- 3 green onions, chopped

1. Take a bowl and add peanut butter, beef stock, amino, lemon pepper, and stir.
2. Keep the mixture on the side.
3. Take a pan and place it over medium-high heat.
4. Add beef, season with salt, pepper, onion powder, and garlic powder.
5. Cook for 7 minutes.
6. Add green bell pepper, stir cook for 3 minutes.
7. Add peanut sauce and green onions.
8. Stir cook for 1 minute.
9. Divide between platters and serve. Enjoy!

Thai Beef with Chilies and Basil (Phat Bai Horapha)

Prep time: 15 minutes | Cook time: 15 minutes | Serves 3

- 1 pound (450g) flank steak, skirt steak, hanger steak, or flap beef, thinly sliced
- 1 tablespoon (15ml) soy sauce,
- 5 teaspoons (25ml) Asian fish sauce
- 1 teaspoon (4g) granulated sugar
- 4 to 6 Thai bird's eye chilies, fresh red or green, divided
- 6 medium garlic cloves, divided
- 1½ tbsp (20g) palm sugar (see note)
- 1 small shallot, thinly sliced
- 4 makrut lime leaves, thinly sliced into hairs (central vein removed), plus more for garnish (see note)
- 2 tablespoons (30 mL) vegetable or canola oil, divided
- 2 cups packed Thai purple basil (approximately 2 oz; 55g)
- Red pepper flakes or Thai chili flakes, to taste(optional)
- ¼ cups fried shallots
- Kosher salt

1. In a mixing bowl, combine the meat, 1 teaspoon soy sauce, 2 teaspoons fish sauce, and white sugar. Toss all together and place in the refrigerator to marinate for at least 15 minutes and up to overnight.
2. Place half of the Thai chilies and garlic in a stone mortar with palm sugar. Using a pestle, grind until mostly smooth paste forms. Mash the remaining fish sauce and soy sauce in a mortar to make a sauce. Place aside. In a small bowl, finely slice the remaining garlic and chilies and mix with the shallot and lime leaves.
3. When you're ready to cook, heat 1 tablespoon oil in a wok over high heat until it begins to smoke. Cook, without moving the beef, until well seared, around 1 minute. Cook, stir, and constantly tossing until the beef is lightly cooked but still pink in spots, around 1 minute. Transfer to a big mixing bowl. Repeat with 1 tablespoon more oil and the remaining beef, moving beef to the same bowl each time. Wipe out the wok.
4. Reheat the wok over high heat and add the remaining beef and the sliced garlic/chili/makrut lime mixture. Cook, tossing, and stirring continuously, for 1 minute, or until the stir-fry is aromatic and the shallots are fully softened.
5. Cook, tossing, and stirring continuously until the sauce mixture is totally reduced in the wok. (The beef should appear moist, but there should be no liquid in the wok.) Toss in the basil right away to mix.
6. Season with salt and optional Thai chili or red pepper flakes to taste. Place on a serving platter. More makrut lime threads and fried shallots on top. Serve with rice right away.

Red Beef Curry

Prep time: 5 minutes | Cook time: 15 minutes | Serves 4

- ¼ cup chopped basil
- ½ cup plus 2 tablespoons coconut milk
- 1 green or red sweet pepper, seeded and cubed
- 1 pound lean beef, cut into fine strips
- 1 tablespoon vegetable oil
- 1–3 tablespoons (to taste) fish sauce
- 2 tablespoons (roughly) ground peanuts
- 2 tablespoons Red Curry Paste
- Rice, cooked in accordance with package directions
- Sugar to taste

1. Heat the oil in a big sauté pan using low heat. Put in the curry paste and cook, stirring continuously, until aromatic, approximately one minute.
2. Mix in the ½ cup of coconut milk and bring the mixture to a simmer. Put in the beef strips and poach for five minutes.
3. Put in the peanuts and continue to poach for another five minutes.
4. Put in the fish sauce and sugar to taste; carry on cooking until the mixture is almost dry, then put in the sweet pepper and basil and cook for 5 more minutes.
5. Serve with rice.

Perfect Pork Dumplings (Khanom Jeeb)

Prep time: 45 minutes | Cook time: 15 minutes | Serves 4

- For Garlic Oil
- 3 tablespoons vegetable oil
- 3 garlic cloves, minced
- For Wonton
- 5 whole black peppercorns
- 2 garlic cloves, peeled, salt to taste
- 2 cilantro stems, chopped
- 5 ounces pork, ground
- 5 ounces minced shrimp
- 5 water chestnut, minced
- 1 tablespoon dark soy sauce
- 1 teaspoon white sugar
- 1 teaspoon fish sauce
- 1 tablespoon tapioca starch
- 1 teaspoon light soy sauce
- ½ tablespoon of salt
- 25 wonton wrappers (or as many as you need)
- Sauce for Dipping
- 3 tablespoons rice vinegar
- 3 tablespoons light soy sauce
- 1 teaspoon white sugar
- 2 scallions, thinly sliced
- 1 bird's eye chili (or more as desired) (Optional)

1. In a small skillet over medium-low heat, heat the vegetable oil and add the minced garlic.
2. Cook until the garlic is golden brown for about 5 minutes. Remove the skillet from the heat.
3. Using a mortar and pestle, crush the peppercorns until they are powdery. Crush peeled garlic and a pinch of salt into a paste. Combine the cilantro stems with the paste.
4. In a big mixing bowl, add the paste, pork, shrimp, water chestnuts, dark soy sauce, 1 tablespoon white sugar, fish sauce, tapioca starch, light soy sauce, and ½ teaspoon salt. Mix well.
5. Fill each wonton wrapper with 1 to 2 teaspoons of the pork-shrimp mixture. Fold the wrapper over the filling to form a purse-like pouch, locking the edges together.
6. Fill a saucepan halfway with water to just below the bottom of a steamer insert. Get a pot of water to a boil. Cover and steam the wontons for about 10 minutes or until the filling is cooked through.
7. In a mixing bowl, combine rice vinegar, light soy sauce, 1 tablespoon white sugar, scallions, and bird's eye chili until well combined.
8. Serve Khanom Jeeb with dipping sauce and a drizzle of garlic oil on the side.

Crying Tiger Grilled Steak

Prep time: 5 minutes | Cook time: 15 minutes | Serves 4

- 2 tablespoons soy sauce
- 2 tablespoons minced garlic (3 or 4 large cloves)
- 1 tablespoon fish sauce
- 2 teaspoons palm sugar, light brown sugar, or granulated sugar
- ⅛ teaspoon ground white pepper or black pepper
- 1 pound boneless steak, such as flank, hanger, strip, rib eye, or flap
- Northeastern Thai Dipping Sauce (here), for serving
- Jasmine Rice (here), for serving
- Optional garnish: sliced shallots, diced tomato, fresh mint

1. In a small bowl, mix the soy sauce, garlic, fish sauce, sugar, and pepper until the sugar is dissolved. Transfer the marinade to a shallow bowl, baking dish, or a resealable plastic bag.
2. Submerge the steaks in the marinade, and place in the refrigerator to marinate for a minimum of 30 minutes (and up to 1 hour).
3. Cook the steaks on a charcoal or gas grill on high, or on an oiled stovetop grill pan over medium-heat heat, to medium-rare, about 140°F on an instant-read meat thermometer, 5 to 10 minutes, depending on thickness of steak and cooking method.
4. Remove from the heat, cover with aluminum foil, and let rest for 5 to 10 minutes.
5. Slice the meat against the grain into thick strips, and serve with the dipping sauce and rice.

Spicy Stir-Fried Beef
Prep time: 10 minutes | Cook time: 10 minutes | Serves 4

- ¼ cup plus 2 tablespoons water, divided
- ½ teaspoon baking soda
- 1 pound boneless beef (such as flank steak), cut against the grain into ½-inch by 2- to 3-inch slices
- 2 teaspoons cornstarch
- 2 tablespoons vegetable oil
- 1 tablespoon minced garlic (2 large cloves)
- 1 small onion, cut into ½-inch wedges
- 1 cup sliced mushrooms
- 2 fresh green Thai bird's-eye, jalapeño, or serrano chiles, stemmed and quartered lengthwise
- 2 fresh red Thai bird's-eye, jalapeño, or serrano chiles, stemmed and quartered lengthwise
- 2 tablespoons oyster sauce
- Jasmine Rice (here), for serving

1. In a medium bowl, mix 2 tablespoons of the water with the baking soda. Add the beef, and toss to coat. Set aside for at least 5 minutes (and up to 15 minutes) to tenderize.
2. Meanwhile, in a small bowl, whisk the ¼ cup water and the cornstarch, and set aside.
3. When the beef is done tenderizing, rinse it well under running water, and drain well.
4. In a large wok or skillet, heat the oil. Add the garlic, and stir-fry until fragrant and light golden, about 30 seconds.
5. Add the beef, and stir-fry until just browned, 2 to 3 minutes.
6. Add the onion, and stir-fry until crisp-tender, 3 to 4 minutes.
7. Add the mushrooms and green and red chiles, and stir-fry until the mushrooms are softened, about 2 minutes.
8. Add the oyster sauce and the cornstarch-water mixture, and stir until the sauce is thickened, about 30 seconds.
9. Serve immediately with Jasmine Rice.

Stir-Fried Beef With Broccoli
Prep time: 5 minutes | Cook time: 10 minutes | Serves 4

- 4 tablespoons water, divided
- ½ teaspoon baking soda
- 1 pound boneless beef (such as flank steak), cut against the grain into ½-inch by 2- to 3-inch slices
- 1 pound broccoli
- 1 teaspoon cornstarch
- 2 tablespoons vegetable oil
- 1 tablespoon minced garlic (2 large cloves)
- 2 tablespoons oyster sauce
- 1 tablespoon soy sauce

1. In a medium bowl, mix 2 tablespoons of the water and the baking soda. Add the beef, and toss to coat. Set aside for at least 5 minutes (and up to 15) to tenderize.
2. Meanwhile, cut the broccoli florets into 2-inch pieces. Peel the stems, and cut crosswise into thin slices.
3. Bring a large pot of water to boil over high heat. Plunge the broccoli (florets and stems) into the water, and blanch just until bright green and crisp-tender, 1 to 1½ minutes. Rinse under cold running water, drain well, and set aside.
4. When the beef is done tenderizing, rinse it well under running water, and drain well.
5. In a small bowl, whisk together the remaining 2 tablespoons of water and the cornstarch, and set aside.
6. In a large wok or skillet over medium heat, heat the oil. Add the garlic, and stir-fry until light golden and fragrant, 30 seconds to 1 minute.
7. Add the beef, and stir-fry until no longer pink, 3 to 4 minutes.
8. Add the broccoli, the remaining 1 cup water, oyster sauce, and soy sauce; raise the heat to high; and bring to a boil.
9. Give the cornstarch mixture a stir, add it to the wok, and simmer until the sauce thickens, about 2 minutes. Serve immediately.

Grilled Ginger Beef

Prep time: 5 minutes | Cook time: 30 minutes | Serves 6

- 1 (2-inch) piece of ginger, minced
- 1 (3-inch) piece ginger, cut in half
- 1 cinnamon stick
- 1 onion, cut in half
- 1 pound green vegetables
- 1 small package of rice noodles
- 2 dried red chili peppers
- 2 stalks lemongrass
- 2 tablespoons (or to taste) soy sauce
- 5 cloves garlic
- 6 (6-ounce) strip steaks
- 6 scallions, minced
- 8 cups low-salt beef broth
- Salt and pepper to taste

1. Put the beef broth, lemongrass, and garlic in a big pot; bring to its boiling point.
2. Meanwhile, put the ginger and onion halves, cut-side down, in a dry frying pan using high heat and cook until black. Put in the onion and ginger to the broth mixture.
3. Put the cinnamon and dried chili peppers in the dry frying pan and toast on moderate heat for a minute; put in to the broth mixture.
4. Lower the heat and simmer the broth for a couple of hours. Cool, strain, and place in your fridge overnight.
5. Before you are ready to eat, remove the broth from the fridge and skim off any fat that may have collected. Bring the broth to a simmer and put in the minced ginger.
6. Soak the rice noodles in hot water for ten to twenty minutes or until soft; drain.
7. Blanch the vegetables for approximately one minute. Using a slotted spoon, remove them from the boiling water and shock them in cold water.
8. Flavour the broth to taste with the soy sauce. Flavour the steaks with salt and pepper and grill or broil to your preference.
9. To serve, slice the steaks into fine strips (cutting across the grain) and put them in 6 big bowls. Put in a portion of noodles and vegetables to the bowls and ladle the broth over the top.

Thai Beef with Rice Noodles

Prep time: 5 minutes | Cook time: 20 minutes | Serves 2-4

- ¼ cup soy sauce
- ½ pound dried rice noodles
- ¾ pound sirloin, trimmed of all fat, washed and patted dry
- 1 pound greens (such as spinach or bok choy), cleaned and slice into ½-inch strips
- 2 eggs, beaten
- 2 tablespoons dark brown sugar
- 2 tablespoons fish sauce
- 2 tablespoons minced garlic
- 5 tablespoons vegetable oil, divided
- Crushed dried red pepper flakes to taste
- Freshly ground black pepper
- Rice vinegar to taste

1. Cut the meat into two-inch-long, ½-inch-wide strips.
2. Cover the noodles with warm water for five minutes, then drain.
3. In a small container, mix the soy sauce, fish sauce, brown sugar, and black pepper; set aside.
4. Heat a wok or heavy frying pan using high heat. Put in roughly 2 tablespoons of the vegetable oil. Once the oil is hot, but not smoking, put in the garlic. After stirring for 5 seconds, put in the greens and stir-fry for roughly two minutes; set aside.
5. Put in 2 more tablespoons of oil to the wok. Put in the beef and stir-fry until browned on all sides, approximately 2 minutes; set aside.
6. Heat 1 tablespoon of oil in the wok and put in the noodles. Toss until warmed through, roughly two minutes; set aside.
7. Heat the oil remaining in the wok. Put in the eggs and cook, without stirring until they are set, approximately half a minute. Break up the eggs slightly and mix in the reserved noodles, beef, and greens, and the red pepper flakes. Mix the reserved soy mixture, then put in it to the wok. Toss to coat and heat through. Serve instantly with rice vinegar to drizzle over the top.

Chapter 6
Chicken

Basil Chicken

Prep time: 5 minutes | Cook time: 20 minutes | Serves 4

- 1 big onion, cut into thin slices
- 1 tablespoon water
- 1½ cups chopped basil leaves, divided
- 1½ tablespoons soy sauce
- 1½ teaspoons sugar
- 2 tablespoons fish sauce
- 2 tablespoons vegetable oil
- 2 whole boneless, skinless chicken breasts, cut into 1-inch cubes
- 3 cloves garlic, minced
- 3 Thai chilies, seeded and thinly cut

1. In a moderate-sized-sized container, mix the fish sauce, the soy sauce, water, and sugar. Put in the chicken cubes and stir to coat. Let marinate for about ten minutes.
2. In a big frying pan or wok, heat oil on moderate to high heat. Put in the onion and stir-fry for two to three minutes. Put in the chilies and garlic and carry on cooking for another half a minute.
3. Using a slotted spoon, remove the chicken from the marinade and put in it to the frying pan (reserve the marinade.) Stir-fry until almost thoroughly cooked, approximately 3 minutes.
4. Put in the reserved marinade and cook for another half a minute. Take away the frying pan from the heat and mix in 1 cup of the basil.
5. Decorate using the rest of the basil, and serve with rice.

Chicken with Black Pepper and Garlic

Prep time: 5 minutes | Cook time: 35 minutes | Serves 4-6

- 1 cup fish sauce
- 1 tablespoon whole black peppercorns
- 1 teaspoon sugar
- 2 pounds boneless, skinless chicken breasts, cut into strips
- 3 tablespoons vegetable oil
- 5 cloves garlic, cut in half

1. Using either a mortar and pestle or a food processor, mix the black peppercorns with the garlic.
2. Put the chicken strips in a big mixing container. Put in the garlic-pepper mixture and the fish sauce, and stir until blended.
3. Cover the container, place in your fridge, and let marinate for twenty minutes to half an hour.
4. Heat the vegetable oil on moderate heat in a wok or frying pan. When it is hot, put in the chicken mixture and stir-fry until thoroughly cooked, approximately 3 to five minutes.
5. Mix in the sugar. Put in additional sugar or fish sauce to taste.

Authentic Chicken Fried Rice (Khao Pad)

Prep time: 15 minutes | Cook time: 10-15 minutes | Serves 4

- To marinate the chicken
- ½ pound thinly sliced chicken
- 1 tablespoon tapioca flour
- 1 tablespoon Golden Mountain Sauce
- To make the Chicken Fried Rice
- 2 eggs, lightly beaten with a pinch of salt
- 1 teaspoon finely chopped garlic
- 5 tablespoons vegetable oil
- 1 onion, chopped sliced coarsely
- ¼ cup fresh serrano or Thai chili peppers, sliced (seeds removed)
- 6 cups Jasmine rice, cooked (made the day before, left at room temp in rice cooker works best)
- 1 tablespoon Golden Mountain Sauce
- 2 tablespoons fish sauce
- 1½ tablespoons Roasted Chile Paste (namprik pao)
- ½ teaspoon salt
- 1 teaspoon lime juice
- 1½ tablespoons sugar
- ½ teaspoon Thai pepper powder
- ½ cup broccoli, cut into small floral florets
- 1 tomato, peeled and cut into wedges
- 2 tablespoons chopped green onion

1. Marinate the chicken in tapioca flour and Golden Mountain sauce for 10 minutes or so.
2. In a wok or skillet, heat 2 tablespoons of oil over medium heat.
3. Allow the eggs to cook before flipping them over and chopping them into smaller pieces with a spatula. Place the egg on a plate and set it aside.
4. Heat the remaining oil in the wok, then add the garlic and cook until golden brown. Stir-fry, the chicken for 3-4 minutes over high heat.
5. Combine the onion, chili pepper, and broccoli in a mixing bowl. Stir all together thoroughly. Pour the next 7 ingredients onto the cooked rice in a separate dish. Add all to the wok gently, stirring carefully to avoid crushing or breaking the rice.
6. Mix all thoroughly. Stir in the tomato, green onion, and egg for about a minute or two. Take the pan off the heat. Garnish with cucumber slices if desired. Have fun!

Stir-Fried Ginger Chichen

Prep time: 10 minutes | Cook time: 10 minutes | Serves 4

- ½ cup dried cloud-ear or wood-ear mushroom (see Note)
- 2 tablespoons soy sauce
- 2 tablespoons fish sauce
- 1 tablespoon oyster sauce
- ½ teaspoon palm sugar or granulated sugar
- 1 pound boneless, skinless chicken (breast or thigh), cut against the grain into bite-size pieces about ¼-inch thick
- 2 tablespoons vegetable oil
- 2 tablespoons minced garlic (3 or 4 large cloves)
- 1 cup sliced carrot
- ½ cup sliced red bell pepper
- 1 (3-inch) piece ginger, peeled and finely julienned into very thin matchsticks
- 4 scallions, cut into 2-inch lengths, white parts also halved lengthwise
- ½ teaspoon sesame oil (optional)
- Pinch ground white pepper or black pepper (optional)
- Jasmine Rice (here), for serving

1. In a medium bowl, soak the mushrooms in enough warm water to cover until softened, about 10 minutes.
2. Meanwhile, in another medium bowl, mix the soy sauce, fish sauce, oyster sauce, and sugar. Add the chicken pieces, and toss to coat evenly. Marinate in the refrigerator for 5 to 10 minutes.
3. Rinse and drain the mushrooms well, and cut them into bite-size slices. Set aside.
4. In a large wok or skillet over medium heat, heat the vegetable oil until shimmering. Add the garlic, and stir-fry just until light golden, 30 seconds to 1 minute.
5. Add the chicken and sauce mixture, and stir-fry until no longer pink, 4 to 5 minutes.
6. Add the mushrooms, carrot, bell pepper, ginger, scallions, and sesame oil (if using), and stir-fry just until the vegetables are softened but still crisp-tender, another 1 to 2 minutes.
7. Sprinkle with the pepper (if using), and serve with Jasmine Rice.

Thai Pineapple Chicken Curry

Prep time: 15 minutes | Cook time: 35 minutes | Serves 4

- 2 cups jasmine rice
- 1 quart water
- ¼ cup red curry paste
- 2 (13-ounce) cans coconut milk
- 2 skinless and boneless chicken breast halves, cut up into thin
- 3 tablespoons fish sauce
- ¼ cup white sugar
- 1½ cups sliced bamboo shoots
- ½ red bell pepper, julienned
- ½ green bell pepper, julienned
- ½ a small onion, chopped
- 1 cup pineapple chunks, drained up

1. Take a pot of water and bring water to a boil.
2. Add rice and lower down the heat to low.
3. Simmer for 25 minutes.
4. Take a bowl and add the curry paste and 1 can of coconut milk.
5. Transfer the mixture to a wok and add the rest of the coconut milk.
6. Add chicken, fish sauce, bamboo shoots, and sugar.
7. Bring it to a boil and cook further for 1 minute until the chicken juices run clear.
8. Take a bowl and mix red bell pepper, onion, and green bell pepper.
9. Add to the wok.
10. Cook for 10 minutes more until the chicken juices run clear.
11. Remove the heat and add pineapple. Enjoy!

Chili-Fried Chicken

Prep time: 120 minutes | Cook time: 20 minutes | Serves 4-6

- ½ teaspoon ground coriander
- ½ teaspoon white pepper
- 1½ teaspoons salt, divided
- 2 small onions, thinly cut
- 2 tablespoons vegetable oil
- 3 pounds chicken pieces, washed and patted dry
- 3 tablespoons Tamarind Concentrate
- 8 big red chilies, seeded and chopped
- Pinch of turmeric
- Vegetable oil for deep-frying

1. In a small container mix the tamarind, turmeric, coriander, 1 teaspoon of the salt, and the pepper.
2. Put the chicken pieces in a big Ziplock bag. Pour the tamarind mixture over the chicken, seal the bag, and marinate minimum 2 hours or overnight in your fridge.
3. In a small sauté pan, heat 2 tablespoons of vegetable oil on moderate heat. Put in the red chilies, onions, and the rest of the salt; sauté for five minutes. Set aside to cool slightly.
4. Move the chili mixture to a food processor and pulse for a short period of time to make a coarse sauce.
5. Drain the chicken and discard the marinade. Deep-fry the chicken pieces in hot oil until the skin is golden and the bones are crunchy. Take away the cooked chicken to paper towels to drain.
6. Put the cooked chicken in a big mixing container. Pour the chili sauce over the chicken and toss until each piece is uniformly coated.

Brandied Chicken

Prep time: 5 minutes | Cook time: 50 minutes | Serves 4-6

- ¼ cup vegetable oil
- 1 (1-inch) piece ginger, cut
- 1 teaspoon salt
- 1 whole roasting chicken, washed and trimmed of surplus fat
- 2 shots brandy
- 2 tablespoons black soy sauce
- 6 tablespoons soy sauce
- 8 cloves garlic, minced

1. Fill a pot big enough to hold the whole chicken roughly full of water. Bring the water to its boiling point using high heat. Lower the heat to moderate and cautiously put in the chicken to the pot. Regulate the heat so that the water is just simmering.
2. Poach the whole chicken for twenty minutes to half an hour or until thoroughly cooked. Cautiously remove the chicken from the pot, ensuring to drain the hot water from the cavity of the bird. Position the chicken aside to cool.
3. Take away the skin from the bird and discard. Take away the meat from the chicken and cut it into 1-inch pieces; set aside. (This portion of the recipe can be done 1 or 2 days in advance.)
4. Put in the oil to a big frying pan or wok and heat on medium. Put in the soy sauces, salt, and garlic. Stir-fry until the garlic starts to tenderize, approximately half a minute to one minute.
5. Put in the chicken pieces, stirring to coat. Mix in the brandy and the ginger.
6. Cover the frying pan or wok, decrease the heat to low, and simmer five to ten more minutes.

Fine Chicken Massaman Curry (Matasaman Curry)

Prep time: 15 minutes | Cook time: 35 minutes | Serves 4

- 2 tablespoons vegetable oil
- 3 tablespoons curry paste
- 1 sliced and minced ginger
- 1 ¼ pound skinless and boneless chicken breast meat, cubed
- 3 tablespoons brown sugar
- 3 tablespoons fish sauce
- 3 tablespoons tamarind paste
- ⅓ cup peanut butter
- 3 cups potatoes, peeled and cubed
- 1 can coconut milk
- 3 tablespoons fresh lime juice

1. Take a large-sized saucepan and place it over medium heat
2. Add oil and heat it up.
3. Add curry paste and minced ginger, stir fry for 2 minutes.
4. Stir in cubed up chicken and cook for about 3 minutes.
5. Stir in brown sugar, tamarind sauce, fish sauce, peanut butter, coconut milk, and potatoes.
6. Bring it to a boil.
7. Lower down the heat to medium-low and simmer for about 20 minutes until the chicken are no longer pink.
8. Add lime juice and cook for 5 minutes more. Enjoy!

Classic Thick Noodle with Chicken (Pad See Ew)

Prep time: 15 minutes | Cook time: 10 minutes | Serves 4

- The Noodle
- 200g dried wide rice stick noodles (7 oz.) or 15 oz fresh wide flat rice noodles (450g) (Sen Yai)
- Apple Sauce
- 2 tablespoons dark soy sauce
- 2 tablespoons oyster sauce
- 2 tablespoons soy sauce (all-purpose or light)
- 2 tablespoons white vinegar (plain white vinegar)
- 2 teaspoons sugar (any type)
- 2 tablespoons water
- Stir-Fried
- 3 tablespoons divided peanut or vegetable oil
- 2 garlic cloves, very finely chopped 1
- 150g / 5oz. boneless, skinless chicken thighs (boneless, skinless), sliced
- 3 tablespoons divided peanut or vegetable oil
- 4 Chinese broccoli stems
- 1 egg

1. Trim the ends of the Chinese broccoli and cut it into 7.5cm/3-inch bits "fragments Separate the leaves from the roots. Thick stems should be cut in half vertically so that they are no wider than 0.8cm / 0.3 "dense.
2. Noodles - Cook and drain according to package instructions. Cook them only before using - if you leave cooked rice noodles lying around, they will break in the wok.
3. Sauce - Combine all of the ingredients in a mixing bowl and whisk until the sugar dissolves.
4. Heat 1 tablespoon oil in a big heavy-bottomed skillet or wok over high heat.
5. Cook for 15 seconds after adding the garlic. Cook until the chicken is mostly white and the color has changed from pink to white.
6. Cook until the chicken is almost finished, then add the Chinese broccoli stems.
7. Cook until the Chinese broccoli leaves are only wilted.
8. Push all to one side, smash an egg into the middle, and scramble. Place all on a plate (scrape wok clean).
9. Return the wok to the stove and heat 2 tablespoons of oil over high heat.
10. Toss in the noodles and sauce. Toss as little as possible to distribute the sauce and caramelize the edges of the noodles.
11. Return the chicken and vegetables to the pan and toss to combine. Serve right away!

Stir-Fried Cashew Chicken

Prep time: 10 minutes | Cook time: 5 minutes | Serves 4

- 1 tablespoon soy sauce plus 4 teaspoons, divided
- ¼ teaspoon baking soda
- 1 pound boneless, skinless chicken (breast or thigh), cut against the grain into bite-size pieces about ¼-inch thick
- ¼ cup oyster sauce
- ½ teaspoon sesame oil
- 1 teaspoon palm sugar or granulated sugar
- 2 tablespoons vegetable oil
- 6 to 8 (2- to 3-inch-long) dried red chiles, stemmed (optional)
- 2 tablespoons minced garlic (3 or 4 large cloves)
- ½ medium onion, cut into ¼-inch slices
- 4 scallions, cut into 2-inch lengths, white parts also halved lengthwise, kept separate
- ½ cup roasted cashew nuts
- Jasmine Rice (here), for serving

1. In a medium bowl, mix 1 tablespoon of the soy sauce with the baking soda. Add the chicken pieces, toss to coat evenly, and transfer to the refrigerator to marinate and tenderize for 10 minutes.
2. Meanwhile, in a small bowl, mix the oyster sauce, remaining 4 teaspoons soy sauce, sesame oil, and sugar. Stir until the sugar is dissolved, and set aside.
3. In a large wok or skillet over medium heat, heat the oil until shimmering. Add the chiles (if using), and stir-fry just until fragrant and slightly browned, but not blackened, 15 to 30 seconds. Remove the chiles from the oil using a slotted spoon, mesh skimmer, or mesh spider, and set aside.
4. Add the garlic to the hot oil, and stir-fry for 30 seconds. Add the chicken, and stir-fry until browned, about 3 minutes. Add the onion and scallion whites, and stir-fry until crisp-tender, about 1 minute.
5. Add the sauce mixture, scallion greens, cashews, and fried chiles, and stir-fry just until all the ingredients are evenly coated in the sauce and the scallion greens are slightly softened, 30 seconds to 1 minute.
6. Serve immediately with Jasmine Rice.

Chapter 7
Fish and Seafood

Baked Redfish with Lime Vinaigrette

Prep time: 5 minutes | Cook time: 10 minutes | Serves 2

- ¼ teaspoon salt
- ½ teaspoon sugar
- 1 clove garlic, minced
- 2 (6-ounce) redfish fillets, washed and patted dry (skate, sole, or flounder also work well)
- 2 tablespoons lime juice
- 2 tablespoons vegetable oil
- 2 teaspoons soy or fish sauce

1. Put the fillets in a shallow baking dish.
2. In a small container, mix the garlic, lime juice, soy sauce, sugar, and salt, then whisk in the oil.
3. Pour the vinaigrette over the fish and bake in a 450-degree oven for six to seven minutes or until done to your preference.

Basil Scallops

Prep time: 5 minutes | Cook time: 5 minutes | Serves 2-4

- ¼ cup shredded bamboo shoots
- ½ pound bay scallops, cleaned
- 1 (14-ounce) can straw mushrooms, drained
- 2 tablespoons vegetable oil
- 3 cloves garlic, chopped
- 3 kaffir lime leaves, julienned, or the peel of 1 small lime cut into fine strips
- 3 tablespoons oyster sauce
- fifteen–20 fresh basil leaves

1. In a wok or frying pan, heat the oil on high. Put in the garlic and lime leaves, and stir-fry until aromatic, approximately fifteen seconds.
2. Put in the scallops, mushrooms, bamboo shoots, and oyster sauce; continue to stir-fry for roughly four to five minutes or until the scallops are done to your preference.
3. Stir in the basil leaves and serve instantly.

Clams with Hot Basil

Prep time: 5 minutes | Cook time: 5 minutes | Serves 4-6

- 1 bunch basil (Thai variety preferred), trimmed and julienned
- 1 tablespoon vegetable oil
- 2 cloves garlic
- 2 pounds Manila clams, cleaned
- 2 small dried red chili peppers, crushed
- 2 teaspoons sugar
- 4 teaspoons fish sauce

1. Heat the oil in a big frying pan on high. Put in the chili peppers, garlic, and clams. Mix the clams until they open, approximately 4 to five minutes. Discard any clams that stay closed.
2. Put in the fish sauce and sugar; stir until well blended.
3. Put in the basil and stir until it wilts.
4. Serve instantly either as an appetizer or with rice as a main course.

Broiled Salmon with 5-Spice Lime Butter

Prep time: 5 minutes | Cook time: 8 minutes | Serves 2

- ¼–½ teaspoon Chinese 5-spice powder
- 1 tablespoon unsalted butter
- 2 (6-ounce) salmon fillets, washed and patted dry
- 2 teaspoons lime juice
- Vegetable oil

1. Using paper towels, wipe a thin coat of vegetable oil over a broiler pan.
2. Preheat your broiler on high, with the rack set on the upper third of the oven.
3. Melt the butter using low heat in a small deep cooking pan. Mix in the 5-spice powder and lime juice; keep warm.
4. Put the salmon on the broiler pan, skin side up. Broil for two to 4 minutes or until the skin is crunchy. Turn the salmon over and broil two minutes more or until done to your preference.
5. Move the salmon to 2 plates and spoon the butter sauce over the top.

Crispy Fluffy Fish and Mango (Yam Pla Dook Foo)

Prep time: 15 minutes | Cook time: 20 minutes | Serves 4

- For the Mango Salad
- Thai chilies, to taste
- 2 tablespoons palm sugar, finely chopped
- 2 tablespoons fish sauce
- 2 tablespoons lime juice
- 12 thinly sliced shallot
- 1 tablespoon dried shrimp, diced
- 1 julienned sour green mango (see note)
- 2 tablespoons cilantro, chopped
- For Fish
- ½ pound any kind of fish meat
- 1 teaspoon soy sauce or a pinch of salt
- 3 tablespoons roasted peanuts
- frying oil

1. Season the fish with soy sauce or salt and steam for 5 minutes or until the meat is completely cooked. If you don't want to steam the fish, you can cook it in whatever way you want as long as you don't get a browned crispy crust on it (poach, bake, even stir-fry in a pan on low heat). When done, allow the fish to cool so you can handle it more easily.

2. Make the mango salad while the fish is cooking and cooling. Pound the Thai chilies in a mortar until there are no more large chunks (chili skin is fine), then add the palm sugar and mash until it's a muddy paste. Swirl in the fish sauce and lime juice until the sugar is fully dissolved. Transfer to a mixing bowl and add the dried shrimp, shallots, and mango. Allow setting while you cook the fish.

3. When the fish has cooled enough to treat, place it in a muslin-lined tub. Wrap the cloth around the fish, twist it to hold the fish in the cloth, and squeeze as hard as you can to get rid of as much liquid as possible (this is why you should let the fish cool; if it's too warm, you won't want to squeeze as hard!).

4. Transfer the fish to a mortar and pestle, and pound it until soft and free of chunks.

5. Heat about 1 - 1.5 inch of oil in a wok or deep pot over high heat to 400°F, and please read and observe the safety precautions above! (Tip: It would be easier to fold the fish if you use a larger pot or wok for this since you will be able to get to it more quickly. Note: For the amount specified in this recipe, you can make two batches of fried fish in a 9-inch-diameter pot.)

6. When the oil reaches temperature, add about half of the fish, and the oil will bubble vigorously. Push the edges of the fish in with a skimmer to clean them up, then leave the fish to fry until golden. I like to force the fish down every now and then so the top is submerged, which helps the fish brown more uniformly. When the fish is golden brown, you can fold it over into a half circle or any shape you like, but this is not needed. Take the fish from the oil with a slotted skimmer and shake it several times to extract the oil that has become trapped inside the fish until the bubbling has slowed and the fish is golden all over. Set aside on a paper towel to drain.

7. Arrange the fish on a plate and top with roasted peanuts. Serve the mango salad alongside the tuna, garnished with chopped cilantro. With jasmine rice, serve. Have fun!

Sardines and Lemon grass

Prep time: 15 minutes | Cook time: 5 minutes | Serves 4

- 2 tablespoons Thai sweet chile sauce
- 1 tablespoon lime juice
- ½ teaspoon kosher salt
- 1 lemon grass, tough outer leaves discarded, and the inner core thinly sliced up
- 1 (3.75-ounce) can sardines, drained and cut up into 1-inch pieces
- 1½ cups lightly packed torn cilantro leaves
- ½ small red onion, sliced

1. Take a large-sized bowl whisk in the chile sauce, lime juice, and salt. Mix well.

2. Add cilantro, lemon grass, sardines, and red onions. Toss well.

3. Transfer to your serving platter and enjoy!

Authentic Seafood Platter (Yam Talay)

Prep time: 15 minutes | Cook time: 10-15 minutes | Serves 4

- For seafood
- 24 small mussels
- 1 tablespoon table salt
- ¾ pound medium (51 to 60 per lb.) new peeled and deveined shrimp
- ½ pound washed squid, sliced crosswise into ¼-inch circles, tentacles cut in half if wide
- ½ pound sea scallops or bay scallops
- ¼ pound jumbo lump crabmeat, fresh or pasteurized
- To make the dressing:
- 6 tablespoons new lime juice (from 2 limes)
- 4 ½ tablespoons fish sauce
- 1 ½ tablespoons granulated sugar
- 2 teaspoons finely chopped unseeded fresh hot green chiles (such as serrano or jalapeno)
- 2 tablespoons finely chopped garlic (2 medium cloves)
- To make the salad:
- 2 cups rinsed and spun-dry bite-size Boston lettuce (1 large head)
- 3 tablespoons thinly sliced shallot (1 large)
- ⅓ cup scallions, thinly sliced (4 to 5, white and green parts)
- ¼ cup fresh cilantro, coarsely chopped
- ¼ cup new mint, coarsely chopped
- ½ cup sliced English cucumber (cut cucumber in half lengthwise and slice into ¼-inch thick half-moons)
- ½ cup cherry or grape tomatoes, halved

1. Scrub the mussels thoroughly under running water and remove any "beards." Any mussels that do not close tightly when tapped on the counter should be discarded.
2. In a medium saucepan, place closed mussels. Pour in around ½ cup water, just enough to reach the bottom of the pan by ¼ inch.
3. Set over high heat, covered. Bring to a boil and cook for 1 to 2 minutes, or until the shells have opened. Remove from the heat, switch to a tray, and leave to cool before you can handle it. Throw away those that haven't been opened. Place the cooked mussels in a medium bowl and remove the shells and cooking liquid.
4. Bring a 3-quart saucepan of water to a boil over high heat to cook the remaining seafood. Return the water to a boil after adding the salt. Pour the shrimp into the boiling water and cook for 2 minutes, or until the largest one is pink on the outside, opaque on the inside, and only cooked through. The water cannot come back to a boil until it is done. Scoop them out with a slotted spoon and place them in the same bowl as the mussels.
5. After the water returns to a rolling boil, add the squid and cook for around 1 minute, or until they become firm and the rings turn bright white. Scoop them out and toss them in with the shrimp and mussels in the tub.
6. When the water returns to a boil, cook the scallops for 1 to 2 minutes for bay scallops and 2 to 3 minutes for sea scallops, or until just cooked through and no longer translucent inside. Scoop them out and place them in the bowl as well (if using sea scallops, you may want to halve or quarter them first).
7. Add the lump crabmeat chunks to the seafood dish. Set the seafood aside on the counter as you make the dressing and other salad ingredients.
8. To make the dressing and salad
9. Combine the lime juice, fish sauce, sugar, chiles, and garlic in a medium-large mixing bowl. Stir to remove the sugar and thoroughly mix everything. Place aside.
10. Assemble the salad as follows:
11. Arrange the lettuce as a bed for the seafood on a big serving platter or individual serving plates.
12. Place the cooked seafood in the bowl with the lime-juice dressing. Add the shallots and gently toss everything together with your hands or a wooden spoon.
13. Mix in the scallions, cilantro, and mint until well combined. Using a slotted spoon, transfer the seafood to the platter or serving plates. Toss the cucumber and tomato in the remaining dressing in the tub, then scatter over the seafood.
14. Drizzle any leftover dressing from the bowl over the salad, paying particular attention to any lettuce that hasn't been covered by the seafood. Serve right away.

Thai Prawn Salad (Pla Gung)

Prep time: 10 minutes | Cook time: 5-6 minutes | Serves 4

- 1 pound prawn tails
- 3 cups water
- 2 tablespoons lemon grass, coarsely chopped
- 1 tablespoon lime leaves, coarsely chopped
- 1 tablespoon coriander leaves, coarsely chopped
- 2 tablespoons lime juice
- 2 teaspoons palm sugar
- 1 teaspoon finely chopped garlic
- 1 teaspoon ginger, finely chopped
- ½ teaspoon ground black pepper
- ½ cup sliced green onions
- ½ cup mint leaves

1. Bring a pot of water to a boil, then add the lemon grass, lime leaves, and coriander. Cook for 5 minutes.
2. Cook for 1 minute after adding the prawns. Remove the item and clean it under cold water.
3. In a mixing bowl, combine lime juice, palm sugar, garlic, ginger, and black pepper. To dissolve the sugar, combine all of the ingredients.
4. Toss the prawns in the dressing to coat. Toss in the green onions and mint leaves.
5. Serve and enjoy!

Poached Fish Fillets In Chili

Prep time: 5 minutes | Cook time: 15 minutes | Serves 4

- 3½ cups water or Basic Thai Chicken Stock (here)
- 2 tablespoons fish sauce
- 1 lemongrass stalk (bottom 3 inches only, bruised with a pestle or the side of a chef's knife)
- 2 thin slices ginger (about ¼ inch thick), bruised with a pestle or the side of a chef's knife
- 1 shallot, diced
- 1 garlic clove, thinly sliced
- 4 boneless, skinless fish fillets (about 6 ounces each)
- Chili, Garlic, and Lime Sauce (here), for serving
- ¼ cup fresh cilantro leaves, roughly chopped

1. In a sauté pan large enough to hold all 4 fillets over high heat, bring the water, fish sauce, lemongrass, ginger, shallot, and garlic to a boil. When it reaches a boil, turn the heat to low, cover, and simmer for 5 minutes to infuse the water with the aromatics.
2. Add the fish, cover, and cook at the barest simmer—only a few bubbles should be visible— until the fish is opaque on the outside but still slightly translucent inside (it will continue cooking for a few minutes after removed from the pan), 5 to 10 minutes, depending on type of fish and thickness of fillets.
3. Remove the fillets from the poaching liquid with a spatula, and serve with the Chili, Garlic, and Lime Sauce spooned on top and sprinkled with the cilantro.

Grilled Squid

Prep time: 5 minutes | Cook time: 5 minutes | Serves 4

- 4 fresh or frozen squid steaks (calamari steaks), about 6 ounces each (see Note)
- 1 cup coconut milk
- 3 tablespoons fish sauce
- Chili, Garlic, and Lime Sauce (here), for serving

1. With a sharp knife, lightly score both sides of each steak in a diamond hatch pattern to prevent them from curling up while cooking.
2. In a large bowl, mix together the coconut milk and fish sauce, and add the squid steaks. Marinate the steaks for at least 30 minutes (and up to 2 hours).
3. Prepare an oiled charcoal or gas grill or an oiled stovetop grill pan over high heat until very hot.
4. Grill the steaks just until opaque, with grill marks, 1 to 3 minutes per side.
5. Serve immediately with the Chile, Garlic, and Lime Sauce for dipping.

Chapter 8
Vegetable Dishes

Asian Grilled Vegetables

Prep time: 60 minutes | Cook time: 8 minutes | Serves 6

- 1 recipe Asian Marinade
- 1 summer squash, cut into 1-inch slices
- 1 zucchini, cut into 1-inch slices
- 12 whole mushrooms, roughly 1-inch in diameter
- 12 whole pearl onions or 12 (2-inch) pieces of white onion
- 2 bell peppers (red, yellow, or green, in any combination), seeded and slice into two-inch squares

1. Alternate the vegetables on 6 skewers (soak the skewers in water until tender if using wooden skewers).
2. Put the skewers in a pan big enough to let them lay flat. Pour the marinade over the skewers and allow it to sit for roughly 1 hour.
3. Put the skewers in a mildly oiled grill basket and place on a hot grill. Cook roughly five minutes on each side or until vegetables are done to your preference.

Curried Green Beans

Prep time: 5 minutes | Cook time: 20 minutes | Serves 4-6

- 1 pound green beans, trimmed Steamed rice
- 2 tablespoons Red Curry Paste
- 2 tablespoons vegetable oil
- 6 cups chicken or vegetable both

1. In a big deep cooking pan, heat the vegetable oil on moderate to high heat.
2. Put in the curry paste and stir-fry for a minute.
3. Mix in the broth until well blended with the paste. Put in the green beans and bring to a low boil. Cook for fifteen to twenty minutes to reduce the liquid.
4. Lower the heat to sustain a hard simmer and carry on cooking until the beans are very well done.
5. Serve the beans over steamed rice, ladling the sauce over the top.

Gingered Green Beans

Prep time: 5 minutes | Cook time: 5 minutes | Serves 2-4

- ¼ teaspoon salt
- ½ cup coconut milk
- ½ pound green beans, trimmed
- 1 stalk lemongrass, minced (inner soft portion only)
- 1 tablespoon peeled and minced ginger
- 1–3 (to taste) serrano chilies, seeded and minced
- 2 tablespoons vegetable oil

1. In a moderate-sized-sized deep cooking pan, heat the oil on moderate to high. Mix in the lemongrass, ginger, and chilies; sauté for one to two minutes.
2. Mix in the coconut milk and the salt until well blended.
3. Put in the green beans, raise the heat to high, and cook for about three minutes or until the beans are done to your preference.

Crunchy Thai Salad with Peanut Dressing

Prep time: 30 minutes | Cook time: 5 minutes | Serves 4

- To Go with the Thai Peanut Dressing
- 1 tablespoon smooth peanut butter
- 2 tablespoons rice vinegar, unseasoned
- 2 tablespoons fresh lime juice (from one lime)
- 3 tablespoons vegetable oil
- 1 teaspoon soy sauce (use gluten-free if needed)
- 2 teaspoons honey
- 2 ½ teaspoons sugar
- 2 cloves garlic, finely chopped
- 1-inch square fresh ginger slice, peeled and roughly chopped
- 1 teaspoon sea salt
- a quarter teaspoon crushed red pepper flakes
- 2 tablespoons cilantro leaves, new
- To Make the Salad
- 4 cups Napa cabbage chopped or shredded coleslaw mix (I like to toss in a little shredded red cabbage for color)
- 1 cup shredded carrots, prepared
- 1 red bell pepper, thinly sliced and diced into bite-sized pieces
- 1 small English cucumber, halved, seeded, and thinly sliced
- 1 cup edamame, cooked and shelled
- 2 thinly sliced medium scallions
- ½ cup chopped fresh cilantro, loosely packed

1. In a blender, combine all of the dressing ingredients except the cilantro and process until fully smooth. Add the cilantro and pulse for a few seconds or until it is finely chopped. Place in the refrigerator until ready to eat.
2. To make the salad, toss together all of the ingredients in a big mixing bowl. If serving immediately, drizzle the peanut dressing over the top and toss; otherwise, serve the dressing on the side to prevent the salad from being soggy

Stir-Fried Baby Mushrooms

Prep time: 10 minutes | Cook time: 15 minutes | Serves 4

- 2 tablespoons olive oil
- 3 garlic cloves, minced
- 1 onion, diced
- 8 ears baby corn, sliced
- ⅔ pound fresh mushrooms, sliced
- 1 tablespoon fish sauce
- 1 tablespoon mild soy sauce
- 1 teaspoon oyster sauce
- 2 tablespoons cornstarch
- 3 tablespoons water
- ¼ cup chopped fresh cilantro
- 1 red chili pepper, sliced

1. In a large skillet or wok, heat the oil over medium heat; cook the garlic in the hot oil until browned, 5 to 7 minutes.
2. Cook until the onion and baby corn are translucent, around 5 to 7 minutes. Cook the mushrooms in the mixture for around 2 minutes or until they are slightly softened.
3. Stir in the fish sauce, soy sauce, and oyster sauce until thoroughly combined.
4. In a small cup, whisk together the cornstarch and water until the cornstarch is dissolved; pour into the mushroom mixture.
5. Cook, constantly stirring until the sauce is thickened and glistening.
6. To eat, move to a serving dish and garnish with chili pepper and cilantro.

Green Beans with Macadamia Nut Sauce

Prep time: 5 minutes | Cook time: 15 minutes | Serves 4-6

- ½ teaspoon cayenne pepper
- ½ teaspoon ground cumin
- ½-1 teaspoon salt to taste
- 1 bay leaf
- 1 cup coconut milk
- 1 medium onion, chopped
- 1 pound green beans, trimmed
- 1 teaspoon ground coriander
- 2 cloves garlic, chopped
- 2 tablespoons vegetable oil
- 2 tablespoons water
- 4 whole raw macadamia nuts, chopped

1. Put the onion, macadamia nuts, garlic, vegetable oil, and water in a blender or food processor and process until the desired smoothness is achieved. Move the paste to a small container and mix in the cayenne pepper, coriander, and cumin.
2. In a moderate-sized-sized deep cooking pan, heat the macadamia nut paste, coconut milk, and bay leaf on moderate to high heat. Heat to a simmer, reduce heat, and cook until reduced to half.
3. Mix in the salt. Put in the green beans and continue simmering, stirring once in a while, until the beans are done to your preference, approximately eight to ten minutes. Put in salt to taste if required.

Cool Stir-Fried Vegetable (Pad Pak Ruammit)

Prep time: 15 minutes | Cook time: 10-15 minutes | Serves 4

- ½ cup broccoli
- ½ cup mange tout
- 1 cup baby corn
- ½ cup carrots, sliced
- ½ cup red pepper, sliced
- ½ cup white mushrooms, sliced
- 1 garlic clove, finely chopped
- ½ tablespoon sugar
- 1 tablespoon soy sauce
- 2 tablespoons oyster sauce
- 2 tablespoons water
- 2 tablespoons sesame oil

1. To make the stir fry sauce: In a mixing bowl, combine 2 tablespoons oyster sauce, ½ tablespoon sugar, 1 tablespoon soy sauce, and 2 tablespoons water.
2. Heat 2 tablespoons of sesame oil in a wok over high heat, then add 1 clove finely chopped garlic and ½ cup sliced carrots and stir fry for 1 minute.
3. To the wok, add ½ cup broccoli, ½ cup baby corn, and ½ cup mange tout and stir fry for another minute or so.
4. Add ½ cup sliced red peppers and ½ cup sliced white mushrooms, followed by the sauce we made earlier. Stir all together for a few minutes more, until the vegetables are cooked to your taste, then serve with steamed jasmine rice!

Lovely Morning Glory Stir Fry (Pad Pak Boong)

Prep time: 10 minutes | Cook time: 2-3 minutes | Serves 4

- 1 pound Morning Glory
- 2-3 Thai chili peppers, new (Or 2 small dried chili peppers)
- 6 garlic cloves
- Stir-Fry Sauce
- 1 tablespoon Korean soybean paste (Doenjang) (Miso Paste is also acceptable!)
- 1 teaspoon Mirim (Rice Wine)
- 1 tablespoon oyster sauce
- ½ tablespoon soy sauce
- ½ tablespoon sugar
- Additional Ingredient for Stir-Frying
- ½ tablespoon soy sauce
- 3-4 tablespoons cooking oil
- a pinch of water

1. Preparation Ingredients
2. Clean Morning Glory thoroughly. Set it in a strainer and let the excess water drain. The stems should then be cut into pinky-finger lengths. Then, cut the leafy part into pointer-finger lengths.
3. Remove the garlic cloves' ends. Then get out your mortar and pestle. Pound the garlic cloves (6) and chili peppers (2-3) together gently. After that, set aside.
4. Stir together the following ingredients to make the Stir-fry Sauce: soybean paste (1 tablespoon), Mirim (1 tablespoon), oyster sauce (1 tablespoon), soy sauce (½ tablespoon), and sugar (½ tablespoon). Thoroughly combine all of the ingredients.
5. Preparing the Meal
6. In a wok or frying pan, heat 3-4 tablespoons cooking oil. Plan on cooking on medium-high heat. When the oil is hot, add the garlic and chili peppers first.
7. Stir-fry until the mixture becomes aromatic. Then add the stems of morning glory. ½ tablespoon soy sauce comes next. For 30 seconds, stir-fry the stems in the soy sauce.
8. Add the leaves after 30 seconds. Then whisk in the rest of the stir-fry sauce.
9. Stir-fry for another 15-20 seconds. Remove from heat and place on a tray.
10. Serve right away with a bowl of hot rice!

Stir-Fried Bok Choy and Sesame
Prep time: 10 minutes | Cook time: 15 minutes | Serves 4

- 2 large bunch Bok choy, cut off, leaves rinsed
- 1 tablespoon sesame oil
- 1 tablespoon olive oil
- 2 whole eggs
- 2 tablespoons low-carb soy sauce
- 1 tablespoon sesame seeds

1. Take a frying pan and place it over medium heat.
2. When the pan is hot, add the sesame seeds and toast till it turns golden.
3. Add olive oil, sesame oil, and soy sauce, then bring to a simmer.
4. Add the Bok choy and stir to coat in oil and soy sauce.
5. Stir the Bok choy continuously as it cooks and wilts.
6. Once done, remove it from the pan and set it aside.
7. whisk eggs to the pan.
8. Scramble them in the remaining soy sauce and oil till just set.
9. Spoon the scrambled eggs over the Bok choy.
10. Serve and enjoy.

Stir-Fried Napa Cabbage
Prep time: 5 minutes | Cook time: 5 minutes | Serves 4

- 1 head Napa cabbage
- 3 tablespoons vegetable oil
- 4 garlic cloves, finely minced
- 1 tablespoon fish sauce
- 1 tablespoon soy sauce

1. Cut the cabbage crosswise into narrow strips (about 1½ inches wide and 3 to 4 inches long).
2. In a wok or large skillet over medium heat, heat the oil. Add the garlic, and stir-fry until light golden, about 30 seconds.
3. Add the cabbage, and stir-fry until crisp-tender, 3 to 4 minutes.
4. Add the fish sauce and soy sauce, stir-fry for about 1 minute more, and serve.

Chapter 9
Rice and Noodles

Broccoli Noodles with Garlic and Soy
Prep time: 5 minutes | Cook time: 15 minutes | Serves 2-4

- 1 pound broccoli, trimmed into bite-sized florets
- 1 tablespoon sugar
- 1 tablespoon sweet soy sauce
- 1-2 tablespoons vegetable oil
- 16 ounces rice noodles
- 2 cloves garlic, minced
- 2 tablespoons soy sauce
- Fish sauce
- Hot sauce
- Lime wedges

1. Bring a pot of water to boil using high heat. Drop in the broccoli and blanch until soft-crisp or to your preference. Drain and save for later.
2. Soak the rice noodles in hot water until soft, approximately ten minutes.
3. In a big sauté pan, heat the vegetable oil on medium. Put in the garlic and stir-fry until golden. Put in the soy sauces and the sugar, stirring until the sugar has thoroughly blended.
4. Put in the reserved noodles, tossing until thoroughly coated with the sauce. Put in the broccoli and toss to coat.
5. Serve instantly with hot sauce, fish sauce, and lime wedges on the side.

Chiang Mai Curried Noodles
Prep time: 5 minutes | Cook time: 5 minutes | Serves 1-2

- ¼ pound ground pork
- ½ cup coconut milk
- 1 tablespoon chopped garlic
- 1 tablespoon curry powder Pinch of turmeric powder
- 1 tablespoon Red Curry Paste
- 1 teaspoon lime juice
- 2 tablespoons fish sauce Pinch of sugar
- 4 ounces rice noodles, soaked in water for twenty minutes to half an hour or until tender Lime wedges, for decoration

1. Heat the coconut milk in a wok or heavy frying pan on moderate heat. Mix in the curry paste and cook until aromatic and a thin film of oil separates out.
2. Put in the garlic and cook for approximately half a minute. Put in the remainingingredients apart from the pork, noodles, and limes, and cook until the sauce thickens slightly, stirring continuously.
3. Put in the pork and continue to stir until the meat is thoroughly cooked. Decrease the heat and keep the sauce warm.
4. Bring a pan of water to a rolling boil. Put the noodles in a wire basket or strainer and immerse the noodles in the water for ten to twenty seconds. Drain the noodles and move to serving plate.
5. Pour the sauce over the noodles. Serve with lime wedges.

Basic Sticky Rice
Prep time: 5 minutes | Cook time: 30 minutes | Serves 2-4

- 1 cup glutinous rice
- Water

1. Put the rice in a container, completely cover it with water, and allow to soak overnight. Drain before you use.
2. Coat a steamer basket or colander with moistened cheesecloth. (This prevents the grains of rice from falling through the holes in the colander.)
3. Spread the rice over the cheesecloth as uniformly as you can.
4. Bring a pan of water with a cover to a rolling boil. Put the basket over the boiling water, ensuring that the bottom of it doesn't come in contact with the water. Cover firmly and allow to steam for about twenty-five minutes.

Coconut Rice (Khao Mun Gati)
Prep time: 5 minutes | Cook time: 15 minutes | Serves 4

- 2 cups jasmine rice, uncooked
- 1 cup coconut milk
- ½ teaspoon salt
- 1 ¾ cups water

1. Rinse the rice well.
2. Take a medium pot and add water, coconut milk, and salt. Place it over medium heat until the salt dissolves.
3. Transfer the rice to the pot. Stir a few times and bring to a boil.
4. Cover the pot and reduce the heat to the lowest setting, and simmer.
5. Keep heating until most of the coconut milk is absorbed for about 15 minutes.
6. Don't open the pot or stir the rice while it's cooking.
7. Remove from the heat, stir a few times with a fork or spatula. Serve and enjoy!

Clear Noodles with Baked Shrimp

Prep time: 5 minutes | Cook time: 30 minutes | Serves 2

- ¼ cup chopped cilantro
- 1 7-ounce package rice noodles
- 1 medium onion, thinly cut
- 1 tablespoon soy or fish sauce Sesame oil to taste
- 1 tablespoon vegetable oil
- 1 teaspoon sugar
- 2 cloves garlic, chopped
- 20–30 black peppercorns
- 6 big shrimp, shell on, washed and patted dry

1. Soak the noodles in hot water until soft, approximately ten minutes. Drain and save for later.
2. Using a mortar and pestle or a food processor, meticulously mix the garlic, cilantro, and peppercorns.
3. Put in the vegetable oil to a wok or big frying pan using low heat. Put in the garlic mixture and stir-fry for a minute. Put in the cut onion and carry on cooking until the onion is soft, then remove the heat.
4. Put in the sugar, soy sauce, and a few drops of sesame oil to the wok; stir until blended. Put in the noodles and toss to coat. Pour the noodle mixture into an ovenproof baking dish. Put the whole shrimp on top of the noodles, cover the dish, and bake for about twenty minutes in a 400-degree oven. Serve instantly.

Basic White Rice

Prep time: 5 minutes | Cook time: 30 minutes | Serves 2-4

- 1 cup long-grain rice (such as Jasmine)
- 2 cups water

1. Put the rice in a colander and run under cool water.
2. Put the rice and the water in a moderate-sized pot. Stir for a short period of time. Bring to a rolling boil on moderate to high heat. Decrease the heat to low, cover, and simmer for eighteen to twenty minutes.
3. Take away the rice from the heat, keeping it covered, and allow it to rest for minimum ten minutes.
4. Fluff the rice just before you serve.

Jasmine Rich

Prep time: 5 minutes | Cook time: 10-20 minutes | Serves 4

- 2 cups uncooked jasmine rice (preferably from Thailand)
- 3 cups water

1. Rinse the rice well Transfer the rice to a medium pot, add the water, stir once or twice, bring to a boil over medium heat, and cover, reduce the heat to very low (the water should be at just a bare simmer), and simmer, undisturbed, until the water is absorbed, generally 10 to 12 minutes for new-crop rice (new-crop rice, generally labeled as such, has a higher moisture content), 15 to 20 minutes for old-crop (any rice not labeled as "new crop" can be assumed to be old-crop). Don't open the pot or stir the rice while it's cooking.
2. Remove from the heat and let rest, covered, 5 to 10 minutes. Fluff the rice with a fork or thin spatula before serving.

Chicken Fried Rice

Prep time: 5 minutes | Cook time: 15 minutes | Serves 4-6

- ¼ cup chicken stock
- ¼ cup dry sherry
- ¼ cup fish sauce
- ½ medium head Chinese cabbage, crudely chopped
- 1 cup shredded, cooked chicken
- 1 cup snow peas, trimmed and slice into bite-sized pieces
- 1 medium onion, cut
- 1 tablespoon minced garlic
- 1 tablespoon minced ginger
- 1 tablespoon vegetable oil
- 2 eggs, beaten
- 3 cups cooked long-grain white rice

1. In a big frying pan or wok, heat the oil on moderate to low heat. Put in the garlic, ginger, and onion, and stir-fry for five minutes or until the onion becomes translucent.
2. Put in the cabbage, raise the heat to moderate, and stir-fry for about ten minutes.
3. Put in the rice and stir-fry for a couple of minutes.
4. Mix the fish sauce, sherry, and stock in a small container; put in to the wok and stir until blended.
5. Put in the snow peas and chicken; stir-fry for a couple of minutes more.
6. Move the rice to the sides of the wok, making a hole in the center. Pour the eggs into the hole and cook for approximately 1 minute, stirring the eggs using a fork. Fold the cooked eggs into the fried rice.

The Original Noodle Soup (Guawy Teow)

Prep time: 15 minutes | Cook time: 20 minutes | Serves 4

- 500 g (1 pound) fresh big rice noodle
- 2 tablespoons lard (or vegetable oil)
- 2 tablespoons divided vegetable oil
- 10 shelled and deveined tiny prawns/shrimp
- 2 finely chopped garlic cloves
- 1 Chinese sausage / Lup Chong sausage, thinly sliced on the diagonal 5 cm / 2"-piece fried fish cake, thinly sliced
- 20 garlic chives leaves, sliced into 4 sections
- 2 ½ cups bean sprouts
- 2 whisked eggs
- 5 tablespoons dark soy sauce
- 4 teaspoons mild soy sauce
- 2 tablespoons oyster sauce
- 4 tablespoons kecap Manis (sweet soy sauce)

1. Combine sauce ingredients well.
2. Do not try to pull noodles apart when they are cold and hard; they may split.
3. Place the entire packet in the microwave and heat on high for 1½ to 2 minutes, or until warm and pliable but not hot, turning the packet over as required.
4. Handle with care and position 500g/1-pound noodles in a heatproof dish. Noodles that have been trapped together must be separated.
5. If the noodles become cold and brittle before cooking, cover with cling wrap and microwave for 30 seconds (not hot, just warm) to avoid breakage.
6. In a large nonstick skillet, heat 1 tablespoon oil over high heat.
7. When the pan is hot, add the shrimp and cook for 1 ½ minutes, or until just cooked through, before transferring to a bowl.
8. Cook for 1 minute, or until the Chinese sausage and fish cake are caramelized, before adding to the dish.
9. Cook, pressing in the edges to create a dense omelet with 1 tablespoon oil. Once it's set, roughly chop it with a wooden spoon (as seen in the video), then add it to the cup.
10. Cook for about 1 minute, or until the bean sprouts begin to wilt, before adding to the bowl.
11. Pour in the lard. When the lard has melted and begins to smoke, add the garlic and immediately add the noodles. Fold gently four times with a spatula and a wooden spoon (as seen in the video) to distribute the oil in the noodles.
12. Return all of the other ingredients, including the chives and whisked eggs, to the pot. Fold gently twice more, then pour over the whole amount of Sauce.
13. Gently toss 4 to 6 times to distribute the sauce, pausing in between to allow the noodles to caramelize on the edges a little.
14. Remove from the heat and serve right away.

Sticky Rich

Prep time: 5 minutes | Cook time: 30 minutes | Serves 4

- 1¼ cups uncooked Thai sticky rice (glutinous rice)
- TO STEAM USING A FINE-MESH STRAINER

1. In a large bowl, soak the rice in enough cold water to cover for at least 4 hours and up to overnight. Drain.
2. In a large pot over medium heat, bring about 2 inches of water to a boil.
3. Place the rice in the fine-mesh strainer (with a lip or hooks that support it on the edge of the pot), place the strainer in the pot over the water, and cover. The water should not be touching the bottom of the rice.
4. Adjust the heat so that the water is at a steady but gentle boil and steam, covered, until the rice is softened, translucent, and sticks together in lumps when pressed, 25 to 30 minutes. It should not be mushy. Flip the rice halfway through cooking using a rubber spatula.
5. Let sit, covered, for 10 to 15 minutes before serving. Keep covered with a damp cloth, or wrapped in plastic wrap, to prevent it from drying out if it will sit for a bit before serving.

Banana Coconut Soup

Prep time: 5 minutes | Cook time: 15 minutes | Serves 6-8

- 1 cinnamon stick
- 1 tablespoon lemon juice
- 2 tablespoons minced gingerroot
- 4 cups banana slices, plus extra for decoration
- 4 cups canned coconut milk
- Salt to taste

1. In a big deep cooking pan, bring the coconut milk to its boiling point. Put in the banana, ginger, cinnamon stick, lemon juice, and a pinch of salt. Decrease the heat and simmer for ten to fifteen minutes or until the banana is very tender.
2. Take away the cinnamon stick and let cool slightly.
3. Using a handheld blender (or a blender or food processor), purée the soup until the desired smoothness is achieved.
4. Serve the soup in preheated bowls, decorated with banana slices and coconut.

Citrus Fool

Prep time: 5 minutes | Cook time: 10 minutes | Serves 4

- ½ cup heavy cream
- ½ cup orange, lime, or lemon juice
- 1 big egg, beaten
- 2 (3-inch-long, ½-inch wide) strips of citrus zest, minced
- 3 tablespoons sugar
- 3 tablespoons unsalted butter

1. Put the juice in a small deep cooking pan. Over moderate to high heat, reduce the liquid by half.
2. Take away the pan from the heat and mix in the sugar and butter. Mix in the egg until well blended.
3. Return the pan to the burner and cook on medium-low heat for three to five minutes or until bubbles barely start to form.
4. Take away the pan from the heat and mix in the citrus zest. Put the pan in a container of ice and stir the mixture until it is cold.
5. In another container, whip the cream until firm. Fold the citrus mixture meticulously into the cream.

Refreshing Thai Iced Tea (Cha Yen)

Prep time: 15 minutes | Cook time: 1 minutes | Serves 1

- 1 tablespoon Thai black tea
- 1 cup hot, scalding water
- 2 teaspoon condensed milk, sweetened
- 2 tablespoons evaporated milk (plus some more to sprinkle on top)
- 2 teaspoons sugar
- 1 cup ice, crushed

1. Bring water to a boil.
2. Fill your tea sock with 1 tablespoon of Thai black tea. It is easiest to place your tea sock in a bowl or large cup to steep the tea.
3. Pour 1 cup of boiling water into the tea sock and gently force it in and out to steep the tea and absorb all of the flavors. Steep the tea for a few minutes or until it has turned a pleasant dark color.
4. Pour 1 glass of hot tea into a fresh cup.
5. Stir in 2 teaspoons of sugar and 2 teaspoons of sweetened condensed milk.
6. Then whisk in 2 teaspoons of evaporated milk, continuing to stir until all is thoroughly combined.
7. Optional - A good Thai iced tea should have some froth or bubbles on top, so take two pitchers and spill the tea from one to the other with a bit of elevation. You might do it differently, but it's a lot of fun!
8. Fill a cup all the way to the top with crushed ice.
9. The gentry Pour your hot tea mixture over the ice in a cup.
10. Drizzle some more evaporated milk on top of your Thai iced tea to add a final creamy touch.
11. With the addition of a straw, you're able to slurp it down!

Bananas Poached in Coconut Milk

Prep time: 5 minutes | Cook time: 10 minutes | Serves 2-3

- ¼ teaspoon salt
- 1 cup sugar
- 2-3 small, slightly green bananas
- 4 cups coconut milk

1. Peel the bananas and slice them in half along the length.
2. Pour the coconut milk into a pan big enough to hold the bananas laid flat in a single layer. Put in the sugar and salt and bring to its boiling point.
3. Reduce the heat, put in the bananas, and simmer until the bananas are just warmed through, approximately 3 to five minutes.
4. Serve the bananas warm on small plates decorated with fresh coconut and pineapple wedges.

Traditional Thai Rice Pudding

Prep time: 15 minutes | Cook time: 25-30 minutes | Serves 4

- 2 cups Thai sweet rice (known as sticky or glutinous rice)
- 3 ½ cups water
- ½ teaspoon salt
- 1 can coconut milk
- ¾ cup palm sugar
- 1 teaspoon vanilla
- 1 teaspoon cinnamon
- ¼ teaspoon nutmeg
- ¼ teaspoon ground cloves

1. Take a large-sized pot with a lid and add 2 cups of water.
2. Add the rice and let it soak for about 10 minutes.
3. Add 1 and a ½ cups of water and salt. Stir well.
4. Place the mixture over high heat and bring it to a boil. Lower the heat to medium-low just as it starts to boil and partially cover the pot with a lid.
5. Boil it as such for 15-20 minutes until the water has been absorbed.
6. Remove the heat and let the rice steam for 10 minutes (by keeping the lid on).
7. Remove the lid and add coconut milk and keep stirring well until fully mixed. Turn the heat to low and simmer it.
8. Add ¾ cup of sugar. Add vanilla, nutmeg, cinnamon, and cloves.
9. Taste it for sweetness and season to your preference.
10. Eventually, the rice will absorb the coconut milk and turn into a nice rice pudding.
11. Garnish with some cinnamon, crushed peanuts, star anise, and serve!

Coconut Custard

Prep time: 5 minutes | Cook time: 60 minutes | Serves 6

- 1 (16-ounce) can coconut cream
- 3 tablespoons butter
- 6 big eggs, lightly beaten
- 1 cup fine granulated sugar
- Fresh tropical fruit (not necessary)

1. In a large, heavy-bottomed deep cooking pan, mix together the coconut cream and the sugar.
2. Over moderate heat, cook and stir the mixture until the sugar is thoroughly blended.
3. Lower the heat to low and mix in the eggs. Cook while stirring once in a while, until the mixture is thick and coats the back of a spoon, approximately ten to twelve minutes.
4. Take away the pan from the heat and put in the butter. Stir until the butter is completely melted and blended.
5. Pour the custard into six 4-ounce custard cups. Put the cups in a baking pan. Pour boiling water into the baking pan until it comes midway up the sides of the custard cups.
6. Cautiously move the baking pan to a preheated 325-degree oven. Bake the custards for thirty to forty minutes until set. (The tip of a knife should come out clean when inserted into the middle of the custard.)
7. Serve warm or at room temperature. Decorate using chopped tropical fruit, if you wish.

Thai Mango Pudding

Prep time: 15 minutes | Cook time: 5 minutes | Serves 10

- 4 mangoes
- 1 cup water
- ½ cup white sugar
- 1½ cups coconut milk
- 4 tablespoons gelatin powder

1. In a food processor, add mangos and pulse to form a smooth puree.
2. Remove the puree from the food processor and transfer to a bowl. Add coconut milk and mix well.
3. In a bowl, add gelatin powder, sugar, and boiled water and stir well.
4. Now mix together the mango and the gelatin mixture.
5. Serve the mixture in serving glasses after cooled.
6. Enjoy!

Classic Thai-style Banana in Coconut Milk

Prep time: 10 minutes | Cook time: 10 minutes | Serves 4

- 3 cups coconut milk
- 2 tablespoons sugar
- 4 bananas, sliced
- Salt, to taste

1. In a saucepan, add coconut milk and bring to a boil.
2. Then add the banana slices in the pan and reduce heat to simmer for about 5 minutes.
3. Season with sugar and salt.
4. Serve in serving glasses. Enjoy!

Tropical Fruit Cocktail

Prep time: 5 minutes | Cook time: 5 minutes | Serves 4

- 2 cans tropical fruit in syrup (options include: rambutan stuffed with pineapple, lychee, jackfruit, longan, sliced toddy palm seed, young coconut, mandarin oranges, or mixed tropical fruit cocktail)
- ½ cup nata de coco (a firm jelly made from coconut) or palm seeds (optional)
- Crushed ice

1. In a medium bowl, mix the undrained cans of fruit, and stir in the drained nata de coco or palm seeds (if using).
2. Distribute evenly, including some syrup, among 4 small serving bowls.
3. Add crushed ice to each bowl, and serve.

Thai-Style Limeade

Prep time: 5 minutes | Cook time: 10 minutes | Serves 1

- 2 tablespoons boiling water
- 4 teaspoons granulated sugar (or to taste)
- Pinch salt
- 4 tablespoons freshly squeezed lime juice (or to taste)
- ¾ cup chilled water
- Ice

1. In a tall glass, pour the boiling water over the sugar and salt. Stir well until the sugar dissolves completely.
2. Stir in the lime juice and the chilled water, and add ice. Stir a few times to chill the drink quickly; adjust the sweetness to your taste, as necessary; and serve.

Thai Iced Tea

Prep time: 5 minutes | Cook time: 10 minutes | Serves 4

- ½ cup Thai tea
- 4 cups water
- ½ cup granulated sugar (or to taste)
- Ice
- 1 cup (or to taste) half-and-half, evaporated milk, milk, light cream, coconut milk, soy milk, or almond milk, divided

1. Put the tea in a large, heat-proof pitcher, bowl, or saucepan.
2. In a medium saucepan over high heat, bring the water to a boil.
3. Pour the boiling water over the tea, stir in the sugar until dissolved, and let steep for 5 to 10 minutes, to your desired strength.
4. Strain through a very fine mesh metal strainer or coffee filter.
5. Divide the tea evenly among 4 tall glasses, add ice, and pour 3 to 4 tablespoons of your choice of milk, cream, or nondairy options over each serving.

Appendix 1 Measurement Conversion Chart

Volume Equivalents (Dry)	
US STANDARD	**METRIC (APPROXIMATE)**
1/8 teaspoon	0.5 mL
1/4 teaspoon	1 mL
1/2 teaspoon	2 mL
3/4 teaspoon	4 mL
1 teaspoon	5 mL
1 tablespoon	15 mL
1/4 cup	59 mL
1/2 cup	118 mL
3/4 cup	177 mL
1 cup	235 mL
2 cups	475 mL
3 cups	700 mL
4 cups	1 L

Volume Equivalents (Liquid)		
US STANDARD	**US STANDARD (OUNCES)**	**METRIC (APPROXIMATE)**
2 tablespoons	1 fl.oz.	30 mL
1/4 cup	2 fl.oz.	60 mL
1/2 cup	4 fl.oz.	120 mL
1 cup	8 fl.oz.	240 mL
1 1/2 cup	12 fl.oz.	355 mL
2 cups or 1 pint	16 fl.oz.	475 mL
4 cups or 1 quart	32 fl.oz.	1 L
1 gallon	128 fl.oz.	4 L

Temperatures Equivalents	
FAHRENHEIT(F)	**CELSIUS(C) APPROXIMATE)**
225 °F	107 °C
250 °F	120 ° °C
275 °F	135 °C
300 °F	150 °C
325 °F	160 °C
350 °F	180 °C
375 °F	190 °C
400 °F	205 °C
425 °F	220 °C
450 °F	235 °C
475 °F	245 °C
500 °F	260 °C

Weight Equivalents	
US STANDARD	**METRIC (APPROXIMATE)**
1 ounce	28 g
2 ounces	57 g
5 ounces	142 g
10 ounces	284 g
15 ounces	425 g
16 ounces (1 pound)	455 g
1.5 pounds	680 g
2 pounds	907 g

Appendix 2 The Dirty Dozen and Clean Fifteen

The Environmental Working Group (EWG) is a nonprofit, nonpartisan organization dedicated to protecting human health and the environment Its mission is to empower people to live healthier lives in a healthier environment. This organization publishes an annual list of the twelve kinds of produce, in sequence, that have the highest amount of pesticide residue-the Dirty Dozen-as well as a list of the fifteen kinds ofproduce that have the least amount of pesticide residue-the Clean Fifteen.

THE DIRTY DOZEN	
The 2016 Dirty Dozen includes the following produce. These are considered among the year's most important produce to buy organic:	
Strawberries	Spinach
Apples	Tomatoes
Nectarines	Bell peppers
Peaches	Cherry tomatoes
Celery	Cucumbers
Grapes	Kale/collard greens
Cherries	Hot peppers

The Dirty Dozen list contains two additional itemskale/collard greens and hot peppers-because they tend to contain trace levels of highly hazardous pesticides.

THE CLEAN FIFTEEN	
The least critical to buy organically are the Clean Fifteen list. The following are on the 2016 list:	
Avocados	Papayas
Corn	Kiw
Pineapples	Eggplant
Cabbage	Honeydew
Sweet peas	Grapefruit
Onions	Cantaloupe
Asparagus	Cauliflower
Mangos	

Some of the sweet corn sold in the United States are made from genetically engineered (GE) seedstock. Buy organic varieties of these crops to avoid GE produce.

Appendix 3 Index

SUNISA KHADPO

Printed in Great Britain
by Amazon

21049151R00045